W9-BTJ-979

• Current Issues in Theology 3 •

• Current Issues in Theology 3 •

The Sources of Theology

Essays on the Theme
with an introduction by
John P. Boyle

edited by
John P. Boyle
and
George Kilcourse

:

The Catholic Theological Society of America
• 1988 •

ISBN 0-86554-331-3

Copyright © 1988
Catholic Theological Society of America
Authorized reprint of plenary essays from
CTSA Proceedings, volume 43 (1988)
with an introduction added
All rights reserved
Printed in the United States of America
Produced for the CTSA by Mercer University Press

∞

TABLE OF CONTENTS

INTRODUCTION

Epochal events like the Second Vatican Council do not occur in a vacuum. However unexpected, such events are the result of earlier developments, some underway for generations before the council met. One such development was the "return to the sources" movement which exerted a powerful influence in the decades immediately preceding the council. Among other things, it gave the impetus to scholars to produce critical editions of source materials available either not at all or in dated and unsatisfactory editions. The new editions made possible scholarly studies which deepened and often corrected our understanding of Catholic doctrine.

Critical study of the development of doctrine is a relatively new phenomenon in the church. But John XXIII opened the Second Vatican Council with an address which explicitly distinguished between the deposit of faith on the one hand and the manner in which it is expressed on the other. In 1973, the Congregation for the Doctrine of the Faith acknowledged in its declaration *Mysterium Ecclesiae* the historicity of the formulations of church doctrine. The council itself introduced changes in the understanding of Catholic doctrine on a number of issues ranging from episcopal collegiality and religious liberty to numerous details of the doctrine of the church.

The period since the council has been a time of continued change. It has also been a time in which the sources of theology have become an important topic of theological discussion. Liberation theologians and others have stressed that the classic sources, scripture and tradition, must somehow be related to the experience of people. There has been tension between theologians and hierarchical teaching authority.

The years since the council have also been marked by a worrisome loss of interest by scholars in the tools, especially languages, needed to keep the classics of the Catholic tradition accessible. And the study of the history of theology seems increasingly to be an interest limited to the few who are specialists. There is concern both inside and outside the academy that the community of Catholic scholars of theology—or at least an important segment of it—is at risk of amnesia, the loss of a knowledge of its own roots, a disease which could threaten the very identity of Catholic theology.

The essays in this collection are therefore timely. They attempt to begin a new conversation among scholars about the sources of Catholic theology, and they invite responses to continue the conversation.

Each of the authors recognized that topic to be treated was too large for comprehensive discussion. Each, therefore, has limited the essay to an aspect of the larger topic. Similarly, each response is necessarily brief and limited in scope.

This third contribution to the series *Current Issues in Theology* will have met its goal if it responds to the lively discussion among Catholic theologians since the Second Vatican Council about theology, its sources, and its relationship to hierarchical teaching authority by inviting theologians to appraise, deepen, and solidify the gains of a quarter century by grounding them in the sources which emerge renewed and strengthened from critical theological scrutiny.

JOHN P. BOYLE
The University of Iowa

THE BIBLE AS A SOURCE FOR THEOLOGY

When your President-elect, John Boyle, first invited me to give an address on "The Bible as a Source for Theology," and then told me that it could last no longer than forty-five minutes, I asked him why he didn't include in the topic "God, the Universe, and Everything Else." A topic like "The Bible as a Source for Theology" naturally called for a sharp narrowing of focus.[1] I had to ask myself: What concrete example in the field of theology today best exemplifies the promises and pitfalls of using the Scriptures as a source for theological reflection?

Of all the possible candidates, the one that intrigues me the most is Latin American liberation theology,[2] with its fierce desire to ground its reflection and praxis in the message and praxis of the historical Jesus, as reflected in the canonical Gospels.

But why choose the use of the historical Jesus by Latin American liberation theologians? For one thing, liberation theologians have brought a breath of fresh air to theology in general and christology in particular. I say this without any disparagement of the fine work done in the area of christology by such first-world scholars as Hans Küng and Edward Schillebeeckx. Schillebeeckx's books, in particular, show an amazing command of a wide range of exegetical opinions, Catholic and Protestant alike. But, for all their newness, Küng and Schillebeeckx still reflect the context of christology as taught in European universities; even the ecumenical sholarship is part of that context.

We seem to breathe a different atomosphere when we turn to the use of "Jesus-research"[3] displayed by Latin American liberation theologians. In saying this, I do not mean to fall into the naive claim that liberation theology is free of academic influence from the first world. Many of the Latin American liberation theologians studied in Europe and/or the United States. To take as examples the the two schol-

---

[1] For a more general consideration of the relation of Scripture to theology today, see J. D. G. Dunn and J. P. Mackey, *New Testament Theology in Dialogue. Christology and Ministry* (Philadelphia: Westminster, 1987). But note that even in this work, the two authors thought it necessary to focus their wide-ranging thoughts on two specific topics: christology and ministry.

[2] Here too the pressures of time and space demand such a limitation of focus. One could easily cast the net farther afield to explore the christology of liberation theologies in other *Sitze im Leben;* see, e.g., in a South African context, Albert Nolan, *Jesus before Christianity* (Maryknoll, NY: Orbis, 1976; 9th printing, 1987).

[3] This is the phrase that James H. Charlesworth prefers to the loaded phrases, "the quest" or "the search for the historical Jesus" (implying that we have lost something that we may or may not find); see his *Jesus within Judaism* (Anchor Bible Reference Library; New York: Doubleday, 1988 [forthcoming]) 1- 2.

ars I intend to study in detail: Jon Sobrino attended St. Louis University and then the Hochschule Sankt Georgen in Frankfurt, while Juan Luis Segundo studied at Louvain in Belgium and the Sorbonne in Paris. Interestingly, their footnotes and bibliographies reflect dependence largely on European rather than U.S. authors. Thus, one does not see the total break with continental scholarship that is sometimes assumed. Sobrino himself points this out in the English-language preface to his early book, *Christology at the Crossroads*.[4]

Yet there *is* a difference as we cross into the third world. The christologies of Sobrino and Segundo have been forged in the furnace of oppression, violence, and the need for a liberating praxis and theology in San Salvador and Uruguay respectively. They represent a fierce drive to make academic theology speak to and be responsible to the lived Christianity of a suffering people yearning for liberation from political, social, and economic enslavement. Within the Catholic Church, no group prior to the liberation theologians had spotlighted so intensely the past misuse of religion to prop up oppressive structures and the need to re-speak Catholic faith and theology to support instead the liberation of the oppressed.

This is a genuine achievement that cannot be gainsaid—least of all by me. If, this evening, I do subject some liberation theologians to the same sort of critique that I have applied elsewhere[5] to Küng and Schillebeeckx, I do so not out of any disdain for Latin America theology. It is all too easy for armchair exegetes in the safety of the United States or Canada to criticize Latin American authors who daily risk their lives by writing with a relevance that could be deadly to themselves. But theologians like Sobrino and Segundo have chosen to write not simply inspiring popular literature and stirring homilies. They have chosen to take up the discourse and trappings of academic sholarship, complete with learned footnotes and references to noted exegetes to bolster their positions and debate their confreres. If, to suppport one's argument, one chooses to play the academic game, then one has to be willing to be judged by the rules of that game. What I propose to do, therefore, is to take a brief look at how a few liberation theologians are incorporating the quest for the historical Jesus into their christologies.

I stress *a few* liberation theologian*s*, since there is no one homogenized liberation theology—as even recent documents from the Vatican have recongized.[6] I do not presume to make judgments valid for all writers in the field. I rather propose to examine the two theologians already mentioned—Jon Sobrino and Juan Luis Segundo—because they are prominent liberation theologians who have recently written specifically on the question of the historical Jesus as the basis of

---

[4]*Christology at the Crossroads* (Maryknoll, NY: Orbis, 1976; ET 1978) xxix.

[5]Notably in a lecture delivered at the Hartford Seminary, Hartford, CT, on 18 March 1988.

[6]So the "Instruction on Certain Aspects of the 'Theology of Liberation,' " issued by the Congregation for the Doctrine of the Faith and dated 6 August 1984 (*Origins* 14 [1984]) 193, 195-204, esp. Section III par. 3 on p. 196: "As with all movements of ideas, the 'theologies of liberation' present diverse theological positions. Their doctrinal frontiers are badly defined." Though the popular press presented this instruction as highly critical of liberation theology, what is perhaps surprising is how much good the Congregation is willing to see in the movement.

liberation theology. Even in such a limited area, though, one cannot presume that an author's opinions have remained unchanged from book to book. Hence I will restrict myself to two recent publications: (1) *Jesus in Latin America,* by Sobrino,[7] with a glance back at his earlier *Christology at the Crossroads;* and (2) *The Historical Jesus of the Synoptics* by Segundo.[8]

I

Sobrino himself, with admirable honesty, warns the reader in his preface to the English-language edition of *Christology at the Crossroads* that there are problems with his use of Scripture: " . . . the scriptural texts introduced in this book stand in need of more solid exegetical grounding, for this particular Christology purports to be based on the historical Jesus." That is the key point for both of these authors: the historical Jesus does not enter in tangentially; he is basic to the whole project. Sobrino continues: " . . . I have tried to take due account of what exegesis has to say about the various passages used here. . . . But the exegetical analysis needs to be worked out in greater detail."[9]

In fact, very few important exegetes are cited at length in *Christology at the Crossroads,* and those who are cited are not the most recent authors. It is symptomatic of the book that Rudolf Bultmann is the most quoted exegete, and often he is referred to more for his general hermeneutics and theology. There are also scattered references to Schnackenburg, Thüsing, Jeremias, Käsemann, and Cullmann, with a few pointers to Bornkamm and Herbert Braun. Notice, by the way, that almost all of these authors are German. The wide range of recent exegetical literature used by Schillebeeckx in his *Jesus* book simply is not there.

But this in not the most serious flaw of *Christology at the Crossroads.* Sobrino's whole presentation of liberation theology claims to be based on the historical Jesus; and that is where it is most seriously lacking. Nowhere in the book is there any extended, critical discussion of what the phrase "the historical Jesus" means or what criteria we are to use to discern authentic material. One almost gets the impression that the historical Jesus equals the full reality of the pre-Easter Jesus, with no awareness of all the difficulties that simplistic equation involves. At times, the historical Jesus seems to be Jesus insofar as he fits into Sobrino's program of liberation theology. For all the talk of a new approach, we are not all that far from the proof-text use of Scripture in the old Catholic manuals of dogmatic theology.

Indeed, Sobrino's work is very much a product of dogmatic and systematic theology, so much so that even when he is speaking about the historical Jesus, most of the writers he cites are German systematicians, especially Rahner, Pannenberg, and Moltmann.

In his more recent book, *Jesus in Latin America,* Sobrino seeks to reply to criticisms of *Christology at the Crossroads.* Unfortunately, the concept of the his-

---

[7]*Jesus in Latin America* (Maryknoll, NY: Orbis, 1987; Spanish original, 1982).

[8]*The Historical Jesus of the Synoptics* (Jesus of Nazareth Yesterday and Today, vol. 2; Maryknoll, NY: Orbis, 1985; Spanish original, 1982).

[9]Sobrino, *Christology at the Crossroads,* xxvi.

torical Jesus continues to remain fuzzy, at times being equated with a christology that emphasizes the humanity of Jesus or Jesus' earthly career.

Even within this fuzzy context there are problems. Sobrino constantly emphasizes Jesus' partisanship and favoritism toward the poor, the oppresed, and sinners. These various groups tend to be lumped together as the object of Jesus' favor, and solidarity with them is seen as the cause of opposition to Jesus and finally of his death. Yet E. P. Sanders, in his fine book *Jesus and Judaism,*[10] points out that it is illegitimate to treat all these groups as one. There is no proof that Jesus' concern for economically poor or uneducated people caused a major scandal or persecution, or was the major reason for his execution. Matters may have been different with his free offer of forgiveness to public sinners who were considered to have broken with Judaism. Here Jesus may have offended *many* sincere and zealous Jews, and not just the rich or powerful. Since such people as tax collectors were not necessarily the poorest members of the community, and indeed some like Zacchaeus (Luke 19:1-10)[11] may have been wealthy, Jesus' scandalous free-wheeling offer of forgiveness to these economic oppressors cannot be simply equated with his care for the economically deprived. (This is a key point, and I will come back to it when I look at Segundo.)

Thus, for all the socioeconomic trappings, Sobrino's treatment of the historical Jesus is socioeconomically naive. What brought Jesus to the cross may have been no one aspect of his ministry, but rather the fact that his ministry offended *so* many groups—including pious Jews—in *so* many different ways that he had few influential supporters when the final clash came between himself and the rulers in Jerusalem over his attacks on the temple. Like Sanders, Sobrino recognizes the importance of the temple question, though he fails to appreciate that such attacks probably alienated not just the Jerusalem priests but also a good many devout Jewish lay people. Just as it is too simplistic to say that all of Jesus' audience was economically poor, so it is too simplistic to say that Jesus offended only the rich and the powerful. Again, I will return to this point when I come to Segundo.

One corollary of these observations is that the precise reason or reasons *why* Jesus was arrested and finally crucified, and the precise grounds on which he was

---

[10]*Jesus and Judaism* (Philadelphia: Fortress, 1985).

[11]I purposely use the phrase "some like Zacchaeus," since this is not the place to enter into a full discussion of the historicity of the Zacchaeus incident. Favorable to at least a historical core are J. Ernst, *Das Evangelium nach Lukas* (RNT; Regensburg: Pustet, 1976) 512-13; J. Fitzmyer, *The Gospel According to Luke (X-XXIV)* (AB 28A; Garden City, NY: Doubleday, 1983) 1218-19; W. Grundmann, *Das Evangelium nach Lukas* (THKNT 3; 7th ed.; Berlin: Evangelische Verlagsanstalt, 1974) 358-59; I. H. Marshall, *The Gospel of Luke* (NIGNTC; Grand Rapids: Eerdmans, 1978) 694-95; M.-J. Lagrange, *Evangile selon Saint Luc* (EB; 4th ed.; Paris: Gabalda, 1927) 487-90; A. Plummer, *The Gospel According to S. Luke* (ICC; Edinburgh: Clark, 1969) 432. Even M. Dibelius hesitates over the question of historicity (*Die Formgeschichte des Evangeliums* [6th ed.; Tübingen: Mohr (Siebeck), 1971] 114-15). R. Bultmann seems in a hopeless minority when he declares the story "an ideal scene, a variant developed out of Mark 2:14" (*Die Geschichte der synoptischen Tradition* [FRLANT 29; 8th ed.; Göttingen: Vandenhoeck & Ruprecht, 1970] 34).

tried, are by no means clear, as Sobrino himself admits.[12] Yet Sobrino proceeds to reconstruct the scenario of Jesus' Jewish and Roman trials, complete with a trial before the Sanhedrin. In all this, Sobrino's theological theses seem to be the guiding rule for deciding what in the Gospel narratives is historical. Once again, we are proof-texting. Having recently spent three days at a colloquium between Christian and Jewish scholars discussing the historical events surrounding the trial of Jesus, I can only marvel at the simplistic treatment Sobrino gives this complex problem. Let me give one example.

While Sobrino, in good Germanic fashion, sometimes omits consideration of the Fourth Gospel from his treatment of the historical Jesus, he does bring in John's Gospel on this question of the persecution of Jesus unto death. Sobrino makes an initial acknowledgment of John's redactional tendencies, but then misses the very point of those tendencies by saying that John makes the whole Jewish people responsible for the persecution of Jesus, and not just their leaders. Actually, the phrase "the Jews" in John's Gospel, when used in a pejorative sense, does not usually mean the whole Jewish people, but rather the hostile authorities in Jerusalem. Worse still, Sobrino proceeds to cite the Johannine texts that refer to the Pharisees' deadly opposition to Jesus and their excommunication of those who acknowledge Jesus as Messiah. Nowhere in all this is there a glimmer of realization that the presentation of the Pharisees as *the* ultimate power in Judaism, before whom even the rulers must tremble, is a post- A.D. 70 picture and hardly reflects the historical Pharisees of Jesus' day. Contrary to Sobrino, the Pharisees probably had nothing to do as a group with Jesus' death. Faced with the horrors of 20th-century anti-Semitism, one should be more careful when dealing with the historical question of who actually was involved in the death of Jesus.

Sobrino's new book, *Jesus in Latin America,* does mark a step forward in his thought, in that he does attempt some definition of what he means by the historical Jesus. The attempt, though, is not auspicious. Sobrino states simply: "Latin American christology understands the historical Jesus as the totality of Jesus' history. . . . "[13] Of course, that is precisely what the historical Jesus cannot be. As

---

[12]It is surprising to see how little discussion there is on the complicated historical question of the trial(s) of Jesus in Sobrino and Segundo. For basic orientation and bibliography, see E. Bammel (ed.), *The Trial of Jesus* (SBT 2d series 13; London: SCM, 1970); O. Betz, "Probleme des Prozesses Jesu," *Aufstieg und Niedergang der römischen Welt* (ed. W. Haase; Berlin/New York: de Gruyter, 1982) II/25.1, 564-647; J. Blinzler, *Der Prozess Jesu* (4th ed.; Regensburg: Pustet, 1969); S. G. F. Brandon, *The Trial of Jesus of Nazareth* (Historical Trials Series; New York: Stein and Day, 1968); R. E. Brown, *The Gospel According to John (XIII-XXI)* (AB 29A; Garden City, NY: Doubleday, 1970) 791-802; D. Catchpole, *The Trial of Jesus* (SPB 18; Leiden: Brill, 1971); M. Hengel, *Crucifixion* (Philadelphia: Fortress, 1977); H. W. Kuhn, "Die Kruezesstrafe," *Aufstieg und Niedergang der römischen Welt,* II/25.1, 648-793; E. Rivkin, *What Crucified Jesus?* (Nashville: Abingdon, 1984); A. Sherwin- White, *Roman Society and Roman Law in the New Testament* (Grand Rapids: Baker, 1963) 24-47; G. Sloyan, *Jesus on Trial* (Philadelphia: Fortress, 1973); A. Strobel, *Die Stunde der Wahrheit* (WUNT 21; Tübingen: Mohr [Siebeck], 1980); P. Winter, *On the Trial of Jesus* (SJ 1; 2d ed. rev. by T. Burkill and G. Vermes; Berlin/New York: de Gruyter, 1974).

[13]"The Importance of the Historical Jesus in Latin American Christology," *Jesus in Latin America,* 65.

Schillebeeckx points out so well in his *Jesus* book, the historical Jesus is that which the methods of historical criticism enable us to retrieve of Jesus of Nazareth.[14] Unlike the positivistic historicism of the 19th century, we must appreciate that what can be reconstructed historically (i.e., the historical Jesus) does not coincide with the full reality of the Jesus who lived in the first century. What really occurs in history is broader than the history recoverable by a historian. As a result, unlike Küng and certainly unlike Sobrino, Schillebeeckx resolutely refuses to identify any or all historical reconstructions with the *real* Jesus—and in this he is methodologically superior. The Gospels hardly give us the totality of Jesus' history, and a quest for the historical Jesus must be highly selective amid the data the Gospels do provide. Hence the *real* Jesus, i.e., the total reality of Jesus of Nazareth as he lived in the first century, is no longer accessible to us by scholarly means. It is this basic insight which touches off a quest for the historical Jesus, and it is this basic insight that is lacking in Sobrino's approach.

Sobrino himself readily acknowledges that Latin American christology has not reflected at length on the methodological problems involved in appealing to the historical Jesus. In the last few pages of his essay on "The Importance of the Historical Jesus in Latin American Christology," he attempts such a reflection. While recognizing that the factual data concerning Jesus are not directly accessible from the Gospels, Sobrino observes that Latin American christology is not especially interested systematically in determining data about Jesus with exactitude. It does not make a christology based on the historical Jesus depend on the *ipsissima verba* or *ipsissima facta* of Jesus. "Its interest rather consists in discovering and historically insuring the basic structure of Jesus' practice and preaching, an end through which the basic structure of his internal historicity and his person are likewise discernible."[15]

Sobrino notes that Latin American christology does not share the radical skepticism of some; rather, it shares "the common heritage of other current christologies (including the European)."[16] Sobrino then proceeds to give a thumb-nail sketch of such a common heritage—and the problem of appealing to such a supposed common heritage becomes evident. The picture is basically that of the Synoptic Jesus: e.g., there is simply one journey to Jerusalem toward the end of Jesus's life. Yet this is mixed up with a strange borrowing from John, namely the idea of a crisis toward the middle or end of Jesus' public life—one element from John that is historically dubious. A good deal of this common heritage is distressingly vague: e.g., Jesus shared "some kind of meal with those close to him" before he was arrested; Jesus showed "certain attitudes toward the Jewish Law and the Temple."[17] Sobrino is no doubt aware that if he gets any more specific than this, his presumed common heritage may evaporate; but without more specificity, these vague snippets are useless.

---

[14]Edward Schileebeeckx, *Jesus. An Experiment in Christology* (New York: Seabury, 1979) 67-71.

[15]"The Importance of the Historical Jesus," 73-74.

[16]Ibid. 74.

[17]Ibid.

In this recent essay, Sobrino does at least examine a few criteria of historicity. Like Harvey McArthur,[18] and unlike Norman Perrin,[19] he finds the criterion of multiple attestation to be the best. Two other criteria, discontinuity with the NT church and the consistency of Jesus' death with what is narrated of his life, are considered indirect verifications of the first criterion.

Yet Sobrino never bothers to use these criteria in any detail. In this there appears a real tension between his awareness of the historical-critical problem and his desire to get on with his project of liberation theology. He states that it is more than likely that the Gospels are in part the fruit of the imagination of the NT communities. But he thinks that it is "rather unlikely" that the Gospels are such in their totality. Then, with a rhetorical wave of the hand, he continues: "At all events, Latin American christology holds a presupposition in favor of the basic historicity of the gospel narratives. . . . To anyone living and suffering history on the South American continent it seems altogether probable that 'Jesus was like that.' ''[20] In short, if it enjoys verisimilitude in the eyes of Latin Americans, it is judged historical.

It is telling that Sobrino admits that his position is a problem from the standpoint of historical criticism, but an advantage from the standpoint of systematic reflection. And that, it appears, is all Sobrino is really interested in. In a sense, Sobrino feels justified in proceeding this way because he is convinced that Latin American communities replicate in their experience the first Christian communities that produced the Gospels. This is simply naiveté once removed. The first Christian communities were by no means all the same in their experience or christology, and to recapture their historical situations is hardly less taxing than recapturing the historical Jesus.[21] In the end, Sobrino substitutes unsubstantiated generalizations for the hard work of Jesus-research. The basic problem is never really engaged, and one is left wondering how, if at all, the Bible has really been a source of theology for Sobrino—or for liberation theology in general.

II

The problem of the historical Jesus certainly *is* engaged—and at great length— by Juan Luis Segundo, who has written a sizable treatise on liberation theology and the historical Jesus. In its English translation, it takes up a whole volume, en-

---

[18]Harvey McArthur, "A Survey of Recent Gospel Research," *Interpretation* 18 (1964) 39-55, esp. 48; idem, "The Burden of Proof in Historical Jesus Research," *Expository Times* 82 (1970-71) 116-19, esp. 118.

[19]Norman Perrin, *Rediscovering the Teaching of Jesus* (London: SCM, 1967) 39- 43.

[20]"The Importance of the Historical Jesus," 74-75.

[21]See, e.g., Raymond Brown and John Meier, *Antioch and Rome* (New York/Ramsey, NJ: Paulist, 1983); Raymond Brown, *The Churches the Apostles Left Behind* (New York/ Ramsey, NJ: Paulist, 1984).

titled *The Historical Jesus of the Synoptics.*[22] To my knowledge, Segundo is the only Latin American liberation theologian who has dedicated an entire book to the question of the historical Jesus.

But precisely because his treatment of the historical Jesus is so much more extensive than that of Sobrino's, the problems of the whole approach become more glaring. At least Sobrino was aware of the deficiencies of his use of Scripture; Segundo seems unaware of the same problem in his own work.

This may sound like a harsh judgment, but time after time throughout *The Historical Jesus of the Synoptics,* Segundo proves to be haphazard and eclectic, as he meshes together and selects from the Synoptics, John, and Paul to construct his portrait of Jesus the political agitator. The more unusual his judgments become, the less he tries to ground them with data and arguments. For example, in justifying Paul's creativity in formulating the gospel message, Segundo says: "Like the authors of the fourth Gospel, the Letter to the Hebrews, and the Book of Revelation, Paul clearly perceives the distance between the historical Jesus and the interpretations of Matthew, Mark, and Luke. So he feels free to create his own gospel . . . " (p. 21). The astounding claim that Paul, writing in the 50's both knew the three Synoptics and perceived their distance from the historical Jesus remains unsubstantiated—as indeed it must.[23] To take another example: although most exegetes point out that John's Gospel lacks any detailed interest in ecclesiology, Segundo declares John the most ecclesial of the Gospels.[24] At times Segundo seems to have an unerring sense for the wrong text to prove his point. To show that Jesus demonstrated partiality toward the poor, Segundo cites the parable of the Pharisee and the publican praying in the temple. The publican, not the Pharisee, goes home justified—fine! But the publican, the tool of the government in extracting tolls or excise taxes, was hardly the economically poorest person in

[22]Juan Luis Segundo, *The Historical Jesus of the Synoptics* (Jesus of Nazareth Yesterday and Today, vol. 2; Maryknoll, NY: Orbis, 1985; ET of the first part [pp. 1-284] of *El hombre de hoy ante Jesús de Nazareth. Vol II/1, Historia y actualidad: Sinópticos y Pablo* [Madrid: Cristiandad, 1982]). While I quote in this article from the English translation, I have compared the English with the Spanish original. Such a comparison reveals some flaws in the translation, but the sentences I consider in detail are present in the same form in the Spanish.

[23]The claim implicit in Segundo's statement goes far beyond the revisionist views proposed by J. A. T. Robinson in his *Redating the New Testament* (Philadelphia: Westminster, 1976) and *The Priority of John* (Oak Park, IL: Meyer-Stone, 1985); and at least Robinson spent hundreds of pages trying to prove his idiosyncratic theories.—Segundo's attitude toward the historicity of the Fourth Gospel oscillates between general rejection and occasional acceptance when it suits his purposes. The same sort of hesitant attitude can be seen in his more recent *Teología Abierta. III. Reflexiones Críticas* (Madrid: Cristiandad, 1984) 35-128, esp. pp. 46-47 and n. 8 on p. 47.

[24]See, e.g., the remarks of Raymond Brown in his *The Community of the Beloved Disciple* (New York/Ramsey/Toronto: Paulist, 1979) 155-62. In my opinion, Brown's mature reflections modify somewhat his views on ecclesiology in the Gospel of John as presented in the first volume of his commentary on the Gospel (*The Gospel According to John* [AB 29; Garden City, NY: Doubleday, 1966] CV- CXI).

Israel, and he belonged on the side of the oppressors rather than the oppressed. If anything, the parable overturns Segundo's, as well as the Pharisee's, theology.[25]

Amid all the confusion, one is relieved when Segundo attempts to articulate a detailed method in treating the historical Jesus—something Sobrino does not do. Segundo enunciates three criteria of historicity: (1) one must distinguish pre-Easter from post-Easter statements;[26] (2) one must distinguish pre-ecclesial from post-ecclesial statements (the criterion of discontinuity); and (3) historicity is supported by multiple attestation. Sad to say, the criteria are not often used in practice. Sayings are often accepted without much reasoning if they fit Segundo's political program; often texts that exegetes would assign to the creative redaction of the evangelists are attributed to the historical Jesus (e.g., Matt 17:12-13, the descent from the mount of transfiguration). The most blatant example of this occurs when Segundo reads Mark's redactional theme of the messianic secret back into Jesus' life. William Wrede must be turning over in his grave.

There is also uncritical meshing of disparate texts. Like some other liberation theologians, Segundo is fond of referring to a Galilean crisis, which seems to result from conflating Peter's confession of faith at Caesarea Philippi in Mark and Matthew with a different profession of faith by Peter at Capernaum in John 6. Indeed, one is left wondering whether Segundo understands his own criteria. He misses the point of the criterion of multiple attestation when he appeals to the fact that a given narrative (e.g., Peter's confession at Caesarea Philippi) appears in much the same way in Mark, Matthew, and Luke. He conveniently overlooks the obvious reason for this agreement, namely, that Mark is *the* source which both Matthew and Luke copied. Hence there is no attestation by multiple *sources*, and no argument for historicity simply from agreement among the three Synoptics.

As one goes through this book, it is not just the portrait of the historical Jesus that becomes increasingly problematic, but also the portrait of historical Judaism in the first century A.D. Instead of a carefully differentiated picture of a highly diverse religion, we get oversimplifications and even caricatures. In practice, for Segundo, the Judaism presented by the four Gospels *is* the historical Judaism of the time of Jesus, period. The recent work of scholars who have investigated the history of first-century Judaism is simply not considered. For example, Segundo claims that among the groups Jesus addressed were the Zealots—ignoring the claims of some historians that the Zealots as a distinct group with that precise name

---

[25]It is true, as Segundo points out in *Teología Abierta. III.*, 90, that publicans could be poor too. Yet it is interesting to notice how, while various people and groups in the New Testament are portrayed as poor (noticeably widows and orphans), no tax collector is every portrayed as poor (cf. Levi throwing a party for Jesus and inviting a large crowd in Mark 2:15). More to the point, nothing in the Lucan parable indicates that the publican is any poorer than the Pharisee; at any rate, the point of the parable hardly rests on such an unsubstantiated assumption.

[26]Actually, this is more of a general principle than an exact criterion that enables one to distinguish authentic from unauthentic material in particular cases. Given the general principle, one must still ask: And how do we know in particular cases what is prepaschal? The individual criteria (e.g., discontinuity, multiple attestation) seek to answer that question. On this point, see also his *Teología Abierta. III.*, 45- 46.

emerged only during the First Jewish War, or at least that they were dormant during the time of Jesus.[27]

Leaning on John's redactional tendencies (esp. chaps. 11 and 18 of the Gospel), Segundo presents the Pharisees and Sadducees plotting together in Jerusalem to arrest and condemn Jesus. Actually, an investigation of the earliest Passion traditions shows that the Pharisees as a group were probably not involved in Jesus' death. The Pharisees are inserted into a few episodes of the Passion by the redactional activity of Matthew and John. Especially disturbing is Segundo's acceptance of Matthew's polemic against the Pharisees in a post-A.D. 70 situation as historically reliable for the time of Jesus. Segundo affirms that the Pharisees are Jesus' enemies par excellence; or better, "they are the enemies par excellence of the God that Jesus reveals. . . . Everything we know about the Pharisees from the Gospels and the extrabiblical sources shows them to be a sincere and fanatically religious group. (Sincerity and fanaticism very often accompany the ultimate stages of bad faith.) Theirs is a terrible legalism. And if they are guilty of hypocrisy . . . , it ultimately stems from hardness of heart . . . , which is translated into an insensitivity to the evident needs of their neighbor. . . . "[28] All one can say is that Segundo is woefully ignorant of all the work done in the last decade or two by both Jewish and Christian scholars to recover a more accurate religious and social description of the Pharisees.

The same criticism can be made of his treatment of the Sadducees. Segundo describes them as follows: " . . . rather than being a sincerely religious sect in opposition to the Pharisees, the Sadducean party seemed to be much more concerned about their own power . . . than about the purity or profundity of their religious opinions."[29] At this point Segundo should have remembered his own hermeneutic of suspicion. Almost everything we know about the Sadducees at the time of Jesus we know from their enemies: the Pharisees, the Essenes, and the Christians. History gets written by the survivors.

In all of this, I am not claiming that Segundo is intentionally anti-Semitic. Rather, I think he lets his reconstruction of first-century history be dictated by his desire to draw parallels between the political oppression of Jesus' day and political oppression in Latin America today. Historical parallels over the chasm of twenty centuries are seldom so simple. Indeed, although Segundo berates exegetes for their lack of concern with the social, political, and economic dimension of the Gospels, he seems unaware of all the work done by North American scholars on the sociology of the NT. This is part of a larger problem; as his notes and bibliographies show, Segundo leans heavily on European exegetes of the 50s and 60s; strictly exegetical works from the 1970s are few and far between—and very few

---

[27]See, e.g., Shaye Cohen, *From the Maccabees to the Mishnah* (Library of Early Christianity 7; Philadelphia: Westminster, 1987) 164-66; Richard Horsley and John Hanson, *Bandits, Prophets, and Messiahs* (Minneapolis: Winston, 1985) 216-43; cf. the earlier article of Morton Smith, "Zealots and Sicarii: Their Origins and Relations," *HTR* 64 (1971) 1-19.

[28]*The Historical Jesus of the Synoptics*, 99.
[29]Ibid. 101.

come from North America. Again, the contrast with Schillebeeckx's wide knowledge of various exegetes is striking.

There is one area in which Segundo's failure to appreciate the Jewish context at the time of Jesus calls his whole political approach into question. This is his treatment of "the poor."[30] One would never guess from Segundo's presentation that "the poor" had long since become more than a mere socioeconomic designation in Palestinian Judaism. Through the spirituality of the Pslams and the prophets, *'ănāwîm,* "the poor ones," along with similar Hebrew adjectives, had become a description of those who had seen through the illusory security of this world and had learned to trust in God alone for their salvation. At times no particular socioeconomic connotation is attached to *'ănāwîm;* a prime example of this can be found in the Book of Ben Sira. In 3:17-18 (for which we have Hebrew fragments), Ben Sira exhorts his audience—presumably the sons of well-to-do in Jerusalem—to walk in *'ănāwâ,* for God reveals his mystery to the *'ănāwîm.*[31]Here the poverty- vocabulary is coming to mean humility, meekness, almost Matthew's "poor in spirit." Indeed, according to some scholars, Matthew's very phrase has now been found in the documents of Qumran (ironically, in the War Scroll!).[32] As the quintessentially pious group, the Essenes called themselves "the poor of God." They provide the prime example of the theology of poverty applied to a whole Jewish sect at the time of Jesus. It may be that the same type of group-designation was applied to the Jerusalem church.[33] I am not arguing here that the vo-

[30]For his treatment of the poor, Segundo relies, among others, on A. Myre, " 'Heureux les pauvres,' historie passeé et future d'une parole," in P.-A. Giguère, J. Marticci, and A. Myre, *Cri de Dieu. Espoir des pauvres* (Montreal: Editions Paulines & Apostolat des Editions, 1977) 67-134; it should be noted that the title of this article is incorrectly given in the bibliography of the English translation, p. 223. Although I admire Myre's work, I would construct the tradition history of the beatitudes in a different way.

[31]For the Hebrew text, with Greek, Latin, and Syriac versions, see *Ecclesiastico* (Pubblicazioni del Seminario di Semitistica, Testi I; Naples: Istituto Orientale di Napoli, 1968) 17; indeed, manuscript A from the Cairo Geniza reads: "My son, *in your wealth* walk in *'ănāwâ*"! The use of *'ănāwâ* for humility can also be found in many Qumran texts, notably the Manual of Discipline (Rule of the Community); see 1QS 2:23- 35; 3:8-9; 4:3; 5:3; 5:24-25; 9:22-23; 11:1.

[32]See 1QM 14:7, where E. Lohse (*Die Texte aus Qumran* [2d ed.; Munich: Kösel, 1971] 212) vocalizes the Hebrew text (unfortunately incomplete) to read *ûbĕ'anwê rûaḥ* ("and by the humble [or poor] of spirit. . . . " This was the reading preferred by J. Dupont in his earlier article, "Les pauvres en esprit," *A la rencontre de Dieu: Mémorial Albert Gelin* (Le Puy: Mappus, 1961) 265-72. Later, however, Dupont changed his view: the Hebrew should rather be vocalized as *'anāwî rûaḥ;* see his "Le ptochoi to pneumati de Matthieu 5,3 et les *'anāwî rûaḥ* de Qumran," *Neutestamentliche Aufsätze* (J. Schmid Festschrift; ed. J. Blinzler, O. Kuss, and F. Mussner; Regensburg: Pustet, 1963) 53-64.

[33]So possibly in Rom 15:26: *eis tous ptōchous tōn hagiōn en Ierousalēm,* though exegetes still fight over whether the genitive is partitive ("the poor members of the Christian community in Jerusalem," so Bultmann, Munck, Georgi, Käsemann) or epexegetical ("the whole Christian community in Jerusalem that constitutes 'The Poor,' " so Lietzmann, Dahl, Bammell, Hahn, Cerfaux).— Granted his own emphasis on the poor, Segundo makes an intriguing point in *Teología Abierta. III.,* p. 122, when he suggests that, speaking anachronistically, Jesus and his disciples came from the lower middle class and were not among the desperately poor of Palestine.

cabulary of poverty had totally left its socioeconomic moorings; many of these people *were* economically poor. I am simply pointing out that the theological use of terms for the poor makes an analysis of the NT data more complex than Segundo claims.

More troubling is Segundo's affirmation, taken over from Joachim Jeremias, that the economically poor and ignorant in Israel (the *'ammê hā-āreṣ*) were viewed as sinners.[34] Jewish scholars rejected such an equation decades ago, and now E. P. Sanders has clearly shown its falsehood in his *Jesus and Judaism*.[35] "Sinners" were the wicked who sinned willfully and heinously and who did not repent; they renounced the covenant. Sinners included people in disreputable professions, such as tax collectors. The scandalous point of Jesus' mission was that he directed himself notably to sinners, i.e., to the wicked. Jesus also was concerned with the poor. But, in Jewish eyes, the damaging charge against him was not that he associated with the poor, but that he associated with the wicked. It is a mistake to think that the Pharisees were upset because Jesus ministered to the ordinarily pious common people and the economically impoverished. There is no passage in the whole of rabbinic literature that states that the super-pious in Israel considered ordinary people to be *ipso facto* wicked. As Sean Freyne has pointed out in his book *Galilee from Alexander the Great to Hadrian*,[36] Galilean peasants were basically loyal Jews, loyal to the Jerusalem temple and to basic tenets and practices of Judaism, though not attracted to the special rules of the Pharisees. In short, Segundo's picture of Jesus' Galilean audience is simplistic and outdated. Not only is he weak in his exegesis, he is weak precisely in his analysis of the religious and socioeconomic situation in Galilee at the time of Jesus.

Segundo's desire to interpret Jesus in a this-worldly political key also leads him to play down or reinterpret those sayings of Jesus which look to a transcendent eschatological future, sayings that imply some divinely caused break with the history of this present world. The rejection of transcendent future eschatology in favor of a restructuring of society in this world is curiously reminiscent of the very founder of the quest for the historical Jesus, Hermann Reimarus.[37] This political interpretation of Jesus has had a long history down to our own day, including notably the books of S. G. F. Brandon, such as *Jesus and the Zealots*[38] and *The Trial of Jesus*.[39] Brandon, like Segundo, denied that Jesus was a Zealot, yet Brandon

---

[34]Joachim Jeremias, *New Testament Theology. Part One. The Proclamation of Jesus* (London: SCM, 1971) 108-13.

[35]*Jesus and Judaism*, 176-79. Segundo repeats the equation of poor and sinners in *Teología Abierta. III.*; see, e.g., p. 78.

[36]*Galilee from Alexander the Great to Hadrian 323 B.C.E. to 135 C.E.* (Wilmington, DE: Glazier, 1980) 208-97. In *Teología Abierta. III.*, 61-62, Segundo makes the startling statement that because Jesus was a Galilean and an artisan, he was looked upon from the start by the religious authorities as a heretic. In general, Segundo too easily retrojects the Judaism of the Mishnah and the Talmud back into early 1st-century Palestine.

[37]Hermann Reimarus, *Reimarus: Fragments* (ed. Charles Talbert; Philadelphia: Fortress, 1970).

[38]*Jesus and the Zealots* (New York: Scribner's, 1967).

[39]*The Trial of Jesus* (Historical Trials Series; New York: Stein and Day, 1968).

thought that Jesus sympathized with the aims of the Zealots. Ernst Bammel shrewdly notes how a number of liberation theologians have become intrigued by Brandon's theory. The whole book in which Bammel's essay appears (*Jesus and the Politics of His Day*)[40] exposes the many difficulties under which Brandon's theory labors; academically, being intrigued by Brandon may prove a fatal attraction. In all this there is a strange irony: While out of touch with the best of recent work on the historical Jesus, especially that of Protestant exegetes, Segundo and his confreres, in a limited sense, have unwittingly reached back to the father of the quest, that great skeptic of the Enlightenment, Reimarus, a Protestant progenitor the Latin American theologians might not care to own. One is reminded of George Santayana's quip that those who are ignorant of history are condemned to relive it.[41]

I fear that my view of the use of Scripture by Sobrino and Segundo may lead some to think that I am simply opposed to liberation theology. That is certainly not the impression I want to leave. I have picked these two liberation theologians for consideration precisely because I admire their personal dedication and scholarly production. I see liberation theology as holding great promise for the renewal of both theology and church life, and I would like to aid it by fraternal correction, not hostile criticism. There is surely room for the former. After all, by the measuring rod of patristic and scholastic theology, liberation theology is still in its infancy and needs to grow in a sophisticated use of the sources of theological reflection—especially the Bible, and most especially that scholarly will-o'-the-wisp, the historical Jesus.

Along with criteria of historicity that must be more carefully defined and employed, I think liberation theologians must rethink a larger christological question: Is it wise, when doing Christian theology, and more specifically christology, to focus so intensely, almost exclusively, on a protean Jesus of history? What is wrong with using, yea, reveling in, the full christology of each of the Gospel writers, whom we affirm in faith to be writing under divine inspiration? Just because I happen to think that Jesus' inaugural homily at Nazareth in Luke 4:16-30 is largely Luke's creative redaction of Mark, or just because I think that the great scene of Jesus judging the sheep and the goats in Matt 25:31-46 owes a great deal to Matthew's creativity, do these inspired texts lack revelatory power as a source for present-day christology and Christian praxis—whether or not the historical Jesus ever spoke them?

Perhaps the liberation theologians are all too quickly going down the primrose path Hans Küng took, the path that naively equates the historical (*geschichtlich*) Jesus with the real (*wirklich*) Christ and then elevates *that* Jesus to the canon within

[40]Ernst Bammel, "The revolution theory from Reimarus to Brandon," *Jesus and the Politics of His Day* (ed. Ernst Bammel and C. F. D. Moule; Cambridge: Cambridge University, 1984) 11-68.

[41]Among the more sophisticated approaches to the social and political framework of Jesus' ministry, see R. Horsley and J. Hanson, *Bandits, Prophets, and Messiahs. Popular Movements at the Time of Jesus* (Minneapolis: Winston, 1985); and R. Horsley, *Jesus and the Spiral of Violence. Popular Jewish Resistance in Roman Palestine* (San Francisco: Harper & Row, 1987).

the canon. The nuanced, differentiated, many-tiered approach of Schillebeeckx is more faithful to the complexity of the biblical witness and the Catholic tradition. It is by embracing, celebrating, and appropriating that complexity that I hope that liberation theologians will make the whole Bible—and the whole Bible's witness to the whole Christ—a true source for their theology.

JOHN P. MEIER
The Catholic University of America

A RESPONSE TO JOHN P. MEIER

Professor Meier's paper makes a provocative beginning for our Society's reflections this year on the sources of theology.

The immediate purpose of his contribution is clear. He acknowledges liberation theology's great promise of renewal for theology and for the life of the church. So he desires to advance it by "fraternal correction"; that is, by pointing out the defects in its use of historical methods as it seeks to ground its program on "that scholarly will-o-the-wisp, the historical Jesus." To make his case concrete and specific, he discusses works of two theologians, Jon Sobrino and Juan Luis Segundo.

His analysis leads him to urge liberation theologians to broaden their base beyond the elusive "historical Jesus"; to draw instead upon the full christologics of the gospel writers; to follow the example of Schillebeeckx in his "nuanced, differentiated, many-tiered approach"; to "make the whole Bible—and the whole Bible's witness to the whole Christ—a true source for their theology."

In its starkest terms, the most significant question posed by Professor Meier's paper is this: Do the methods of historical criticism hold a veto power over anything which liberation theologians (or any other theologians, for that matter) may say about the "historical Jesus"?

I take it that Professor Meier would answer "Yes" to this question; that, in his view, such a veto power is the prerogative of historical criticism. For he not only argues that Sobrino and Segundo fail to meet the requirements of historical method in their portraits of the historical Jesus. He proceeds to charge Sobrino with "proof-texting" and Segundo with being "haphazard and eclectic." This, of course, is academic language which denies and dismisses the value of another's work.

Therefore, when they speak of the "historical Jesus," may responsible theologians now say only what can pass through the sieve of historical criticism? If so, an impasse— indeed, an unbridgeable chasm—necessarily separates the liberation theologians from the exegetes.

On the one hand, our Latin American colleagues are not likely to accept Meier's "fraternal correction" nor his proposal that they broaden their base beyond the historical Jesus. As elusive as he may be, Sobrino and Segundo are not about to surrender the "historical Jesus" as the basis and starting point of their christologies. They know only too well that dehistoricized Christs have been turned into idols which tolerate and even legitimate suffering in Latin America.[1] More-

---

[1]Jon Sobrino, *Jesus in Latin America* (Maryknoll: Orbis, 1987; original, 1982) 58-59.

over, they love Jesus too much to allow that religious manipulation to continue.[2] From their perspective, Meier's offer to help looks a lot like a Trojan horse.

On the other hand, who pays serious attention to "proof-texters," to those whose work is haphazard and eclectic? Theology that ignores fundamental demands of scholarship contributes nothing to authentic renewal. Those who acknowledge the indispensable contributions of historical criticism to contemporary theology will ignore liberation theologians like Sobrino and Segundo if they are guilty of these accusations. But then the great promise of Latin American liberation theology will not be fulfilled.

Perhaps the chasm can be bridged and the promise of liberation theology undimmed if we broaden our perspective on this debate. I suggest that Sobrino and Segundo are not inept amateurs in the academic game they have chosen to play. Rather, they are engaged in systematic theological reflection which, like all such reflection today, is based on a number of different but mutually related sources. These sources include but are not limited to the results of historical investigation.

In the nature of the case, footnotes do not disclose all the sources of a particular theological work. Footnotes may be downright misleading. They may purport to be comprehensive, but they cannot delineate precisely that critically important source for theology of which we have become acutely aware in our own time: experience—both individual and cultural.

Now the experience which constitutes the distinctive characteristic and source for Latin American liberation theology is a suffering which beggars description in kind and number. Those who suffer are not only a major source for liberation theology but they are also its primary audience.[3] When we North Americans read liberation theology, we are overhearing an anguished communal exploration of the good news Jesus embodies and proclaims. Those explorers attend to but refuse to be governed by what Professor Meier calls "the rules of the academic game." Injustice, oppression, suffering, and death: these constitute the main lenses through which the Gospels are read in Latin America, not the methods of historical criticism.

But then should the Latin Americans always check their understanding of Jesus revealed by suffering against the Jesus revealed by historical criticism to insure the accuracy of their portrait? If they do not, are they shoddy in their work or guilty of making Jesus the instrument of their political programs? Not necessarily.

Historical methods are important but limited in their scope. The issue of their role and limits became inescapable for Roman Catholicism in the so-called

---

[2]Ibid. 12.

[3]Thus, for example, Sobrino: "It may be that the reader will find here some theoretical advance: a stronger emphasis on relating Jesus not only to the kingdom of God but also to the God of the Kingdom, a new effort to root faith in Jesus in the faith of the church in Christ. This certainly is my aim. But my aim has been above all to foster clear vision and bold courage in Christians who follow Jesus, who seek conversion, who battle for justice by struggling with oppression, who defend the cause of the poor and the oppressed. If these writings help these Christians a little, they will have more than fulfilled their purpose" (xiv; see also 10).

"Modernist crisis." In an illuminating correspondence with Alfred Loisy, Maurice Blondel argued that "the accumulated experience of generations of Christians and my own intimate experience" were reliable sources of knowledge of Jesus, in addition to historical methods.[4] More recently, David Tracy has proposed that theologians today can and do believe in "the Resurrection of Jesus on the basis of some personal religious experience of Jesus Christ as the crucified and risen one."[5]

These necessarily undeveloped suggestions mirror the age-old and constant conviction and practice of the church itself. The Risen Jesus who is called upon in prayer, followed in discipleship, recognized in the breaking of the bread (Luke 24.35), and present in the church until the end of time (Matt 28.20) is also he who proclaimed the Kingdom of God from Galilee to Jerusalem and there was crucified under Pontius Pilate. Thus, Vatican II reminds us, "it is not from Sacred Scripture alone that the Church draws her certainty about everything which has been revealed" (*Dei verbum* 9).

Now if the methods of historical criticism do not provide the only access to the historical Jesus, if there are other forms of mediation (collected under the rubric of "Tradition" in *Dei verbum* 8) which yield reliable knowledge of him, the importance of historical criticism is certainly not negated. It is, however, relativized insofar as its methods and conclusions need to be brought into dialogue with the methods and conclusions of other mediations of the historical Jesus. The goal is a theology not less critical but more so.

The dialogue envisioned here would enrich liberation theology and North American theology as well. There are good reasons for the dominance of historical methods among those available to contemporary theology. Yet there are also good reasons why this dominance must not become a dictatorship. We can help liberation theology advance not by asserting a veto power for historical methods but by entering into dialogue with an eagerness to learn. For our Latin American sisters and brothers claim to encounter Jesus in "places" unfamiliar to us, the poor and suffering.[6] They are confident in speaking about the historical Jesus in light of these encounters. If we listen carefully, perhaps we can collaborate with them in finding the ways to translate their knowledge into theology which squares with the canons of contemporary scholarship.

In a dialogue like this, we too could learn much. Few of us have mastered the art of translating our North American faith communities' experiences of Jesus into terms and genres that satisfy the requirements of scholarship. All too often our attempts come off as privatized, sectarian, or voluntaristic. It is not too much to

---

[4]See Richard J. Resch, *Christology as a Methodological Problem: A Study of the Correspondence Between Maurice Blondel and Alfred Loisy, 1902–1903* (Ann Arbor: University Microfilms, 1979) 175.

[5]David Tracy, "To Trust or Suspect," *Commonweal* 111 (1984) 533.

[6]Sobrino identifies the places of the real encounter with Christ as liturgy, preaching, the community of believers and the "unequivocal place of encounter with Christ," the poor and oppressed of whom Matthew 25 speaks.

hope that our dialogue with Latin America will help us to meet some of the theological challenges we face here in North America.

JON NILSON
Loyola University of Chicago

THE HISTORY OF THEOLOGY:
FORTRESS OR LAUNCHING PAD?

To speak of the history of theology as a source of theology may provoke quite different reactions from theologians situated at opposite ends of the methodology spectrum. At one extreme we might find theologians who would agree with French President François Mitterand's dictum: "Nothing is more important than history." At the other extreme we might find theologians who would prefer the pithy remark of Henry Ford, Sr.: "History is bunk!" Let me hasten to say that while one of the places where I teach is the Pontifical Institute of Mediaeval Studies, one of our founders, Étienne Gilson, always held that the act of existing is crucial philosophically and theologically—and that means existing not in the historical past but at this moment; following him, I would not accept Mitterand's dictum literally. I was also much influenced by working with Marie-Dominique Chenu, whom I consider one of the greatest theologians of our century. Chenu was able to move back and forth between the history of medieval theology on the one hand, and contemporary theology and sociology on the other; for him each area illuminated his research in the others. So successful was he that one seminary rector, who had to introduce him for a conference to his seminarians, thought there were two different Chenu's, one the medievalist and the other the avant-garde theologian, and he wasn't sure which one he had present to introduce! On the other hand, were I to agree with Henry Ford that history is bunk, in this city that houses the *Lonergan* Centre, I would be troubled by the wraith and wrath of that great theologian: for in a seminar here at the Institute of Mediaeval Studies Lonergan introduced me to historical-textual studies of Aquinas' Trinitarian theology; and, far more importantly, in his *Method in Theology* he carefully examined the third functional specialty, history and, within the specialty of doctrines, the historicity of dogmas.

The historicity of dogmas and the historicity of theology: that is perhaps the place to start our considerations. The growth of historical consciousness, together with the development of critical history, sociology, ethnology, and social psychology, has convinced most theologians that all truth is grasped in an historically conditioned way, that therefore dogmatic statements and theology are historically conditioned. How could it be otherwise when human persons and societies work out their destiny through time and history, when they achieve their personal and social identity through historical memories that give them meaning in the present and that thrust them into their futures? In this respect some may be surprised by the conclusions of an essay by my colleague, Armand Maurer, who has shown that for Thomas Aquinas "there is no room . . . for *created* ETERNAL truths, for this would imply that God could give truths eternal being, which is reserved to him alone,"[1] and that for Aquinas "the discovery of truth itself has a temporal and historical dimension."[2]

Many recent studies have taken up this question.[3] Karl Rahner, in an essay published posthumously in 1985, speaks indeed of his "rather cool relationship to the history of dogma" (not, however, to the history of theology). But despite his reservations, he declares emphatically: "The history of faith-consciousness is not at its end, and its future will always be brought about *in company with* reflection on what has gone before. This is self-evident for a historical religion, which is something other than a metaphysics with its tendency to eliminate its historical conditioning as much as possible."[4]

To follow the historical development of any theological theme helps us to see how the mystery of God and of God's saving work transcends the conceptual and institutional frameworks that developed through history. The history of theology can liberate us from excessive attachment to the concepts and even the questions of our own day; it can help us to see the relativity of our human analogical concepts with relation to the fundamental mysteries that can never be adequately expressed. It is a liberating and at the same time a humbling discipline. At the outset of our investigation, then, we can say that the very historicity of truths, as well as the historicity of human persons and societies that bear and develop these truths,

---

[1] "St. Thomas and Eternal Truths," *Mediaeval Studies* 32 (1970) 91-107; this quotation is from 105: emphasis mine.

[2] Ibid. 106. In this article Maurer shows that early modern discussions of the nature of eternal truths were influenced by the Suarezian metaphysics of essence rather than by Aquinas' doctrine of esse."

[3] Before Lonergan's *Method,* several studies of the late 1960's had already examined this question, among them: Winfried Schulz, *Dogmenentwicklung als Problem der Geschichtlichkeit der Wahrheitserkenntnis,* Analecta Gregoriana, 173 (Rome: Univ. Gregoriana, 1969); George Vass, " On the Historical Structure of Christian Truth, I & II," *Heythrop Journal* 9 (1968) 125-42, 274-89; *Truth and the Historicity of Man: Proceedings of the American Catholic Philosophical Association* 43 (Washington, Catholic Univ. of America, 1969); *Neuntes Forschungsgespräch: Geschichlichkeit der Theologie,* ed. Thomas Michels (Salzburg-Munich: Anton Pustet, 1970); more recently, *Dogmengeschichte und katholische Theologie,* ed. Werner Löser, Karl Lehmann, and Matthias Lutz-Bachman (Wurzburg: Echter, 1985).

[4] See his "Dogmengeschichte in meiner Theologie," in *Dogmengeschichte,* 323-28. The quotation, from p. 325, reads as follows in the original: "Die Geschichte des Glaubensbewusstseins ist nicht zu Ende und ihre Zukunft wird immer auch durch eine Reflexion auf die Vergangenheit *mit*bewirkt. Das ist für eine geschichtliche Religion, die etwas anderes ist als eine Metaphysik mit ihre Tendenz, ihre geschichtlichen Bedingtheiten nach Kräften auszuschalten, selbstverständlich" (emphasis his). He adds (ibid.): "Die Lehre der Schrift und der Glaube der Väter bleiben immer eine wesentliche Norm für das Glaubensbewusstsein der Kirche, auch für jededenkbare Zukunft. Und darum muss das Glaubensbewusstsein, wie es in der Schrift und in der darauf folgenden Tradition gegeben ist, präsent bleiben, also immer wieder neu erforscht werden." Rahner's reservation is about the possibility of new dogmas being formulated from within the history of *dogmas* (a problematic that perhaps reflects Rahner's own somewhat baroque scholastic historical conditioning), but he speaks very positively about the role of the history of *theology,* ibid. 326-28, in ways that are somewhat akin to our own.

require us to look to the history of theology as a source of contemporary theology. We cannot begin theology in a state of amnesia.

But how is the history of theology to be used as a source? Before coming to that, a couple of distinctions are in order. First, the *history of theology* is not, as I see it, the same as *historical theology,* although the two have been and are confused by some.[5] Historical theology I understand to be a method of doing contemporary theology by reflecting on past theology and its historical contexts. It is, I believe, the important second step to be taken, but only after we have taken the first step, that is, only after we have carefully investigated past theology and its contexts. The distinction between them may be compared to that between exegesis and interpretation of biblical texts on the one hand and the hermeneutic that helps make the past texts come alive with meaning in the present. The historical theologian first reflects on what she or he has learned from the history of theology—and this already involves a good deal of interpretation, with all its problems. From this reflection he or she then develops insights that are significant for today's theology. This paper is, in fact, such an exercise in historical theology: it is not a study or interpretation within the history of theology, although examples will be given; rather, it attempts to reflect on the history of theology itself and the past use of this history in order to gain some insights—insights related, in this case, to contemporary method in theology.

A second distinction. "Source" or "sources" of theology may be understood in two ways. The first meaning has some background in certain texts of Augustine, in some twelfth-century theologians;[6] and in some important texts of Aquinas;[7] it equates "source of theology" with a *topos* or *locus* adapted from rhetoric. For Cicero, depending here on Aristotle, a *topos* or *locus* meant the basis or foundation (*sedes*) on which to build an argument.[8] Using Cicero, in part through the influence of Rudolph Agricola [Roelof Huysman], Melchior Cano systematized

---

[5]Examples from the past: William Cunningham, *Historical Theology: A Review of the Principal Doctrinal Discussions in the Christian Church since the Apostolic Age,* 2 vols. (Edinburgh 1867 for vol. 2), which is basically a history of doctrines; John Stoughton, *An Introduction to Historical Theology: Being a Sketch of Doctrinal Progress* (London: n.d., 19th c.), which has some concluding reflections on the history of doctrines described; more recently, Geoffrey W. Bromily, *Historical Theology: An Introduction* (Grand Rapids: Eerdmans, 1978), a history of doctrines and theologies, and the title "Bulletin de théologie historique" used in the *Revue des sciences philosophiques et théologiques* for what is basically a review of works in the history of theology.

[6]Yves Congar, *La foi et la théologie* (Tournai: Desclée, 1962) 143, lists Abelard, Hugh of St. Victor, and Robert of Melun; he relies on Grabmann, De Ghellinck, and E. R. Curtius.

[7]Especially *Summa theologiae* I, q. 1, a. 8 ad 2m.

[8]See *Topicorum,* c. 2: "Sic enim appellatae ab Aristotele sunt hae quasi sedes quibus argumenta promuntur. Itaque licet definire locum esse argumenti sedem"; and *Orator,* c. 14: "Aristoteles . . . locos sic enim appellat, quasi argumentorum notas tradidit, unde omnis, in utramque partem, traheretur oratio." Quoted by Gardeil in "Lieux théologiques," *Dictionnaire de théologie catholique* 9/1 (1926) col. 716; whole article, cols. 712-47.

the various *loci* according to ten divisions.[9] Cano's work was at the head of a movement using these sources to *prove,* or at least to qualify by theological "notes," the degree of certitude of dogmatic and theological propositions. This use tended to be rather narrow, juridical, and almost casuistic.[10]

The other meaning of "sources of theology" is much more general than the first; it is the one used in the last fifty years or so in phrases such as "return to the sources" or "ressourcement." Yves Congar speaks about sources in this sense as "organs that communicate truth and life in truth, organs that are coextensive with the building up of the Church."[11]

In speaking of the history of theology as one of the sources of theology, I want to take "sources" in this broader sense. This means that in speaking of it as a source, I am understanding the history of theology, as Congar puts it, "as situated in an overall theology of the Church, of knowledge by faith, and of Tradition."[12]

Earlier I mentioned biblical and historical interpretation and hermeneutics. This topic brings in a whole complex of questions and problems that are indeed related to both the history of theology and historical theology. (It could be the entire topic of this paper, but I will only mention a few points and leave that area open for discussion afterwards.) First, I agree with Bernard Lonergan, who admits that the techniques of critical history cannot eliminate historical relativism *totally* but who nevertheless goes on to say, "I affirm all the more strongly that [these techniques] can and do effect a partial elimination."[13] Lonergan holds that this partial escape

---

[9]*De locis theologicis* (Salamanca, 1563), Agricola's work, *De inventione dialectica,* was published at Cologne in 1527 and at Paris in 1529. For his influence on Cano, as well as that of Cicero see Gardeil, cols. 714-22.

[10]This is Yves Congar's judgment in *La foi et la théologie,* 143: "Depuis lors, ce traité a été mis au point, non sans une focalisation de l'attention sur le magistère, et même le magistère romain. Il a pris souvent aussi une allure dialectique, juridique, presque casuistique, faute d'être situé dans une théologie d'ensemble de l'Église, de la connaissance de foi et de la Tradition." Although there is this danger of theology degenerating into trying to prove theses by appeals to various levels of authority precisely as authorities (as in the old manuals of theology), theological notes do have an important pastoral use in helping to distinguish what is truly of faith from what is taught by the Church or even by the body of theologians but is not a matter of faith. Failure to make this distinction clear in catechisms and preaching has led to constant worries among many in the church that changes in official teachings that are not of faith are contrary to faith. For some of these changes see my article, "When 'Authentic' Teachings Change," *The Ecumenist* 25/5 (July-August 1987) 70-73.

[11]Ibid. 143-44: "Pourtant, que sont les 'lieux' (si l'on tient à garder cette expression), sinon les médiations, diverses et dégradées, par lesquelles, en deçà de la Parole, Dieu instruit et édifie son Église? Il ne s'agit pas seulement ici de références scientifiques diversement qualifiées, mais des organes d'une communication de vérité et d'une vie dans la vérité, qui sont coextensives à la construction de l'Église."

[12]See the quotation above, n. 10.

[13]*Method in Theology* (New York: Seabury, 1972; 2nd ed., 1973; paperback, 1979) 195: emphasis mine. That relativism can be partially overcome is clear from two examples: (1) the difference between a poor and a good edition of a patristic or medieval text that arises from an editor's poor or good knowledge not only of the language and subject of the text,

from relativity is made possible by what he calls the "ecstatic" aspect of historical inquiry. By "ecstatic" he means that when new data and new questions arise, a historian who acts with probity is led by the new data and questions to "stand out from," that is, to modify previous assumptions and perspectives.[14]

At the same time, modern hermeneutical discussions have alerted us to the problems in interpreting history generally and the history of theology in particular. For instance, the hermeneutics of suspicion has led theologians to investigate the masculine and patriarchal bias of ecclesiastical documents and theology; it has led liberation theologians to question doctrinal decisions and theological positions supporting privileged groups in society. Along these lines, a recent study of the medieval theology of the papacy led me to such a hermeneutics of suspicion regarding the views of some of my own favorites, Bonaventure, Albert, Aquinas, and other Mendicant theologians. That is, I was led to ask whether their strong advocacy of universal papal power in teaching and jurisdiction arose at least partially from the fact that the Mendicants were the popes' favored communities, with special privileges for preaching and teaching, privileges that at times brought them into conflict with pastors and university teachers in the local churches. These and other hermeneutical principles need to be applied universally to past conciliar documents, to past official pronouncements, indeed to all the works of past theologians.[15] This makes the task of historians of theology and historical theologians more difficult, almost forbidding; yet for my part I wish I were near the start of my career in order to do more of this work because I think it is one of the most exciting and liberating movements in contemporary theology.

Leaving this vast problem for now, we turn to the title of this paper. It asks whether, as a source of theology, the history of theology is a fortress or a launch-

---

but also from how extensive is his or her knowledge of the different contexts that influence the text; (2) the illumination of historical events or doctrines that comes with a historian's corrections of previously held positions by new research, these corrections finding general acceptance in the scholarly community that is knowledgeable about the matter.

[14]Ibid. 187-88: "Now if one is on the right track long enough, there occurs a shift in the manner of one's questioning for, more and more, the further questions come from the data rather than from images based on surmises. One still has to do the questioning. One still has to be alert. But one has moved out of the assumptions and perspectives one had prior to one's investigations. One has attained sufficient insight into the object of one's inquiry to grasp something of the assumptions and perspectives proper to that object. . . . To describe this feature of historical invesiagtion, let us say that the cumulative process of datum, question, [188] insight, surmise, image, formal evidence, is ecstatic. It is not the hot ecstasy of the devotee but the cool one of growing insight. It takes one out of oneself. It sets aside earlier assumptions and perspectives by bringing to light the assumptions and perspectives proper to the object under investigation." Interesting reflections on and application of hermeneutical principles are to be found in a recent article by John W. O'Malley, "Priesthood, Ministry, and Religious Life: Some Historical and Historiographical Considerations," *Theological Studies* 49/2 (June 1988) 223-57. In the same issue, the articles by Jacques M. Gres-Gayer ("The *Unigenitus* of Clement XI: A Fresh Look at the Issues," 259-82), and by Mary Ann Donovan ("Alive to the Glory of God: A Key Insight in St. Irenaeus," 283-97) also demonstrate the importance of fresh interpretations of past documents.

[15]See below, p. 33 and n. 35.

ing pad. The image of a fortress is meant to raise the question whether using the history of theology as a source of theology can be compared to certain uses of a fortress or castle. Ancient and medieval rulers used fortresses for security, for defence against attacking enemies; it was a place where those who possessed title, territory and wealth could protect their goods, a place from which they could sally forth to attack invaders. Fortresses could be good or bad things. Preserving territories, cultural goods, and the very lives of people against destroying marauders such as Norsemen or Muslims would certainly be good for those who accepted the rule of the castle dwellers. But fortresses and castles could also be used to bolster positions of privilege, to resist social change, to exploit those less privileged persons who were governed by the castle rulers: how readily, when it was possible, did so many serfs leave feudal estates to swell the population of the burgeoning cities of the twelfth and thirteenth centuries. The history of theology, I think, has been used as a source for a theology like a fortress in both a good and a bad sense.

The launching-pad metaphor means to raise the question whether using the history of theology as a source of theology can be compared to employing those bases from which human explorers travel into outer space to search for new truths about the universe and indeed the human condition. Can the history of theology serve today to stimulate, to open new horizons, to raise questions from the past that lead to insights about the present and even the future? I shall contend that indeed it can, that this is its most important contribution to theology. However, launching pads and the equipment launched from them can also be dangerous and, as we have seen only recently, they can even be fatal to the explorers. And if they are used to launch atomic missiles, they are deadly and destructive of others. So, too, research in the history of theology and use of it as a source for contemporary theology, if not properly conducted, if not correctly employed for good purposes, if not ecstatic in Lonergan's sense, can be harmful in theology and church life.

Let us explore the fortress image first. The history of theology has been used, I believe, as a fortress sometimes in a bad sense and sometimes in a good sense. In the bad fortress sense, the history of theology has sometimes been invoked to maintain certain authoritative or theological teachings in the face of legitimate inquiry and new developments. In particular, it has been used (a) for polemical purposes against theological opponents; (b) to bolster new decisions by overstating the witness of the past; (c) to try to maintain continuity, apparent or real, in authentic Catholic teaching; and (d) to maintain the status quo. I shall give examples of each, drawing mostly on areas where I have done some work.

An example of polemical use of past theology against opponents can be found in the Second Council of Constantinople's condemnation of the Three Chapters (Theodore of Mopsuestia [†428], Theodoret of Cyr [†ca.466], and Ibas of Edessa [†ca.457]), who had been dead for nearly or more than a century. This judgment of theologians of the past was part of the drive of Justinian and eastern bishops to attack Antiochene Christology and, to some extent, the Council of Chalcedon.[16]

---

[16]See articles in the various encyclopedias on 'Three Chapters,' the 2nd Council of Constantinople, Monophysitism, and the three theologians who were condemned. E.g., F. X. Murphy, "Three Chapters," *New Catholic Encyclopedia* 14 (1969) 144-45; *The Oxford*

In this case past theology was unjustly used for a present purpose—unjustly used, we now know, because modern scholarship generally holds that these theologians were orthodox (many at the time said the same and opposed the condemnation). Indeed, Pope Paul VI, by quoting Theodore as a patristic authority (albeit on the Eucharist), seems to have rehabilitated Theodore as orthodox.[17]

This, by the way, is but one instance of a long-standing bad fortress use of the history of theology for polemical purposes. To put down an adversary and maintain one's position, nothing could be better than unfairly to find in his or her positions hints of heresies or errors such as Arianism, Nestorianism, Monophysitism or, in our day, "a fundamental Marxist option."[18]

Another example of this kind of polemic use would be amusing if it were not so sad. In 1058 Cardinal Humbert of Silva Candida went on a mission to the East on behalf of Rome. After debating points of difference between the Eastern and Western Churches, the exasperated cardinal excommunicated the patriarch, Michael Cerularius. In doing so, he accused the Greeks of daily sowing heresies: you are, he charged, like simoniacs, Valesian Gnostics, Arians, Donatists, Nicolaites. He even charged them with having cut the *Filioque* out of the Creed![19]

Dictionary of the Christian Church, 2nd ed., eds. F. L. Cross and E. A. Livingstone (Oxford: University Press, 1974, rpt. with corrections, 1978). "The Three Chapters" referred at first to certain *kephalia* (chapters) of their writings but soon came to be applied to the persons, that is "the three subjects condemned by the Emperor Justinian in an edict of 543-44, viz. (1) the person and works of Theodore of Mopsuestia, (2) the writings of Theodoret against Cyril of Alexandria, and (3) the letter of Ibas of Edessa to Maris. As all three were considered sympathetic to Nestorius, Justinian issued the edict in the hope of conciliating the Monophysites by a display of anti-Nestorian zeal" (ibid. 1375).

[17]See his encyclical on the Eucharist, *Mysterium Fidei,* in *Acta Apostolicae Sedis* 57 (1965) 571: "His verbis S. Ignatii Antiocheni licet addere ea quibus Theodorus Mopsuestenus, hac in re fidei Ecclesiae testis fidelis, populum est allocutus: Dominus enim non dixit: Hoc est symbolum corporis mei, et hoc symbolum sanguinis mei, sed: *Hoc est corpus meum et sanguis meus.* Docet nos non attendere naturam rei subiectae ac sensibus propositae: ea enim per gratiarum actionem et verba super eam pronuntiata, in carnem et sanguinem mutata est" (*In Matth. Comm.,* c. 26; PG 66:714). (English translation in *The Pope Speaks* 10 [1965] 320.) Although the pope says that Theodore is a faithful witness "on this point," the *stylus Romanae curiae* would forbid his being quoted at all as an authority in anything if he were stilled considered heretical in his christology. This also seems to be a historical correction of the Council by the pope. See also a letter of Paul VI to Cardinal Willebrands, *Acta Apostolicae Sedis* 66 (1974) 620-25, especially 622-23, for an example of Paul VI's freedom in criticizing past councils. He blames the intransigence and lack of sensitivity to Greek concerns on the part of western representatives at the 2nd Council of Lyons (1274) for the quick failure of the union reached at that council between East and West. (French translation of the letter in *Documentation Catholique* 72, no. 1668 (19 January 1975) 63-65. This is an example of how present history of theology can help to correct past views and to teach lessons for the present.

[18]The last is the judgment of Cardinal Ratzinger concerning liberation theology. See my forthcoming article in *Franciscan Studies,* "Catholicity, Inculturation, and Liberation Theology: Do They Mix?"

[19]See *Excommunicatio qua feriuntur Michael Caerularius atque ejus sectatores,* ed. Cornelius Will (Leipzig, 1861; rpt. Frankfurt am Main: Minerva, 1963) 153-54. He says

An example of the use of past theology to bolster new magisterial teaching can be seen from a working seminar, soon to be published, that was recently held at the Pontifical Institute of Mediaeval Studies. The seminar dealt with the religious ideal of the papacy between 1150 and 1300. Taking only that relatively short time span, we saw that proponents of absolute papal primacy and universal jurisdiction buttressed their views with appeals to the history of theology that would be considered dubious today. They narrowed the differing patristic and medieval interpretations of the Petrine scriptural texts to the one that favored papal supremacy; they misapplied the image of the two swords; they skewed the metaphor of marriage between Christ and the church: Innocent III pushed the metaphor to the extent of declaring himself, as successor of Christ, the Bridegroom of the Church, and comparing the Church of Rome to Sarah, Abraham's wife, and the other local churches to Hagar, the slave girl brought in to Abraham to bear children. They also replaced the title "Vicar of Peter" with the title "Vicar of Christ" and as such "Head of the Church."[20] Many of these developments continued later and were used to enhance Vatican I's teachings on the papacy, teachings that found liturgical application when Pius XII established a special common for popes in the liturgy, something quietly eliminated and hardly missed after Vatican II's reform of the liturgy.

Another example of past use of theology for support was the Council of Trent's decrees on original sin and purgatory. The fathers of this council bolstered their statements not only about the main doctrine, but also about many details of original sin, by saying that they were following "the witness of sacred scripture and of the holy fathers and of the most trustworthy councils as well as the judgment and consent of the Church" (DS 1510). The doctrine of Purgatory, they added, is taught from the sacred writings and the ancient tradition of the fathers in the sacred councils (DS 1820). It would be difficult, it seems to me, to find the details of either doctrine as expounded by the council in the scriptures or with any unanimity in the Fathers (one thinks of the different approach of the eastern and western Fa-

---

(153): "Quantum autem ad Michaëlem abusive dictum patriarcham, et ejus stultitiae fautores, nimia zizania haereseon quotidie seminantur in medio ejus. Quia sicut Simoniaci donum Dei vendunt; sicut Valesii hospites suos castrant, et non solum ad clericatum sed insuper ad episcopatum promovent; sicut Ariani rebaptizant in nomine sanctae Trinitatis baptizatos, et maxime Latinos; sicut Donatistae affirmant excepta Graecorum ecclesia ecclesiam Christi et verum sacrificium atque baptismum ex toto mundo periisse; sicut Nicolaitae carnales nuptias concedunt et defendunt sacri altaris ministris; sicut Severiani maledictam dicunt legem Moysis; sicut Pneumatomachi vel Theumachi absciderunt a symbolo Spiritus sancti processionem a Filio. . . . "

[20]See *The Religious Roles of the Papacy: Ideals and Realities, 1150-1300*, ed. Christopher Ryan (Toronto: Pontifical Institute of Mediaeval Studies, 1988 or 1989), for essays by Karlfried Froehlich (on the exegetical tradition) and by myself (on the school theologians' teachings, and on the monastic, episcopal, and apologetic theology of the papacy). A certain pattern also emerged in these studies: those seeking reform of local abuses, but finding it difficult or impossible to achieve reform, would often appeal to the pope to intervene, justifying his intervention by exalting the pope's power and authority. Such requests, together with subsequent papal interventions, done with the best intentions, nevertheless tended to subject local churches more and more to the central papal authority.

thers on original sin, and of the strong influence of the particular Augustinian teaching on it in the West).[21] As for the theme of original sin in our time, it seems that particular historical theological views about the transmission of original sin influenced Pope Pius XII, in his encyclical *Humani Generis* of 1950, to reject the possibility that there was more than one pair of first human ancestors (DS 3897).

Another concern, that of maintaining continuity of doctrine, even in matters not of faith, has led to a similar fortress use of past theology. Thus in christology a strong but relatively late western theological tradition held that Christ's human knowledge included the beatific vision; this tradition influenced the Holy Office in 1918 to insist that Christ had beatific knowledge, that he knew in the Word everything that God knows by knowledge of vision, and that in Catholic schools one was not allowed to teach a limited human knowledge in Christ (DS 3645-47). In 1943 Pius XII maintained and further specified this western tradition by saying that "through that blessed vision by which, scarcely conceived in the womb of the God-bearer, [Christ] enjoyed bliss, he had all the members of his Mystical Body continually and perpetually present to himself, and embraced them with his saving love" (DS 3812).

With respect to maintaining continuity of teaching, John Maxwell notes in his study on slavery that "the common Catholic teaching concerning the moral legitimacy of slavery was not corrected before 1965." One of many reasons for this, he says, was "the overriding influence of the principle of continuity of doctrine. Popes, bishops, canonists and moralists in the eighteenth and nineteenth centuries could not easily accept that a moral doctrine which had been commonly taught for over 1,400 years could possibly be mistaken."[22]

Another fortress use of the history of theology, this time to maintain the status quo, is well known because it is so recent and so evidently intended to prevent any consideration of change. I refer to the document on the question of womens' ordination. Here both scripture and tradition, viewed through a particularly narrow historical lens, are invoked to reject such ordination. It is argued, first, that Christ ordained only men,[23] even though we have to ask the historical question whether Christ himself actually ordained the Twelve or some group of apostles or indeed anyone to a ministerial order distinct from the service he expected of all his fol-

---

[21]On the other hand, it is interesting to see that the Council does appeal as well to the "judgment and consent of the Church."

[22]*Slavery and the Catholic Church* (London, 1975) 13.

[23]Sacred Congregation for the Doctrine of the Faith, *Declaration on the Question of Admission of Women to the Ministerial Priesthood* (Vatican City: 15 October 1976) 6: " . . . The Church, in fidelity to the example of the Lord, does not consider herself authorized to admit women to priestly ordination. . . . But over and above considerations inspired by the spirit of [patristic] times [that is, the writers recognize some anti-feminine prejudices in some Fathers], one finds expressed — especially in the canonical documents of the Antiochian and Egyptian traditions — this essential reason, namely, that by calling only men to the priestly Order and ministry in its true sense [!], the Church intends to remain faithful to the type of ordained ministry willed by the Lord Jesus and carefully maintained by the Apostles." See also no. 2 (p. 6): "Jesus Christ did not call any women to become part of the Twelve."

lowers, or whether ordination to such a distinct order developed only in the early church.

Second, it is argued that in the subsequent history of the church women have not been ordained priests, so that unchangeable tradition holds that such ordination is impossible today or in the future.[24] What amazes me about this appeal to unchanging tradition is how clearly opposed it is to the notion of a living, developing tradition that theologians have had to produce when speaking about Mary's Immaculate Conception or Assumption, or when defending the definitions concerning the papacy. The history of theology and the notion of tradition seem to be able to be manipulated to fit the purposes of those who hold the fortress.[25]

These are a few examples of what I consider to be bad fortress use of the history of theology as a source. But I think the good side of the fortress image should also be pointed out. Fortresses or castles not only preserved status and privilege; they also served a good purpose by preserving lives, valuable possessions, and cultural treasures. It seems to me that the history of theology, as a source of theology, can function like a good fortress or castle in an analogous way.

The first such good use is the history of theology's recalling the unanimous or quasi-unanimous agreement of the Fathers and the early church on fundamental points of doctrine. This use of the history of theology, however, is becoming more and more difficult to sustain as we come to know the Fathers better. We observe the considerable time span covering them, the historical changes within these times, the great varieties in their cultural contexts, their diverse responses to theological problems, and their own distinctive theologies. In fact, I have been toying with the question whether this notion of a common consent among the Fathers is not a chimera. It does seem to me, however, that the consensus reached by the Fathers and received by the early church on some basic doctrines can stand as a fortress preserving fundamental truths of Christianity and can help Catholic theologians to avoid useless by-paths. Although hermeneutical principles must be employed to make these doctrines meaningful today, I would include among them the belief that the Father, Son, and Holy Spirit are not each other and yet are one God; that the Word or Son of God is the subject in a fully human Christ; that Christ rose from death in a bodily but transformed state; that original sin is a real evil and not the mere negation of supernatural elevation; that Christ's body and blood are present in the Eucharist, however this presence is explained.

Another point. We theologians generally like to proceed unhampered in our research, and any talk of limitation or restriction is not very popular. But must we not admit that one task of theology is to defend against errors that have evil pastoral effects? Think of the Gnostic doctrines that endangered the early church. Think of how the church has had to fight Docetism, Manicheism, and other related views in order to protect the goodness of marriage and of the human body. Think of the

[24]See ibid. nos. 3-4 (pp. 8-11).

[25]I proposed a study of these conflicting notions of tradition as a topic for the International Theological Commission, but the suggestion met with the same silence that greeted another suggestion, a reexamination of the ecumenicity of the councils since the split between East and West.

early church's fight against fate and her insistence on human free will. In our day, think of the inroads of fundamentalist preachers on TV and in Latin America, or of Shirley MacLaine and the New Age brand of religiosity, to say nothing of astrology or of California friends of a president's wife. In meeting these contemporary errors, the history of theology can be helpful. Although, as I have said, the history of theology can be used to tag opponents unfairly with heretical labels, it can also give us models of theological positions of the past that can alert us to corresponding affinities in present-day ideas.

A more positive "fortress" use of the history of theology leads into the launching pad theme. As a fortress, the history of theology preserves for contemporary theologians an abundance of riches that can be forgotten. When the study of the history of theology recalls these riches, it can and often does launch researchers into new theological skies. Proof of this is found in the return to sources that began toward the end of the last century, a return that issued in the biblical movement, the liturgical movement, changes in theological methodology, and finally the Second Vatican Council. Louis Bouyer has said that an incipient liturgical movement in the seventeenth century failed for lack of solid historical research, whereas the more recent one grew successfully out of decades of solid preparatory studies.

Thus the history of theology has launched theologians into new orbits with respect to *methodology*. Whereas the decadent neo-scholastic theology of the textbooks seemed to ape the deductive methods of the sciences, the study of the Fathers and of monastic and other spiritual authors of the middle ages has helped theologians to recall the value of symbolism, rhetoric, metaphor, and other literary techniques. Chenu has written a stimulating article on literature as a theological "place." He points out how the Fathers and some medieval authors were able to bring their theology into vital symbiosis with their culture because they used literary techniques; he blames later scholastics, who imitated Wolff, for the isolation of theology from culture in recent centuries.[26] Again, in the 1940's there was an intense controversy in France and Italy between traditional neo-scholastic theologians and those espousing a "new theology" that employed a wide range of historical studies. The arguments against the introduction of history and new methods into theology seem quaint and obscurantist today, given the evident fruits of these new methods.

Turning from methodology to individual theological *themes,* we can say that in practically every theological theme the history of theology can help to launch theologians into new explorations and insights. I should like to dwell on four themes that examine what I think are some of the most crucial problems facing the church and so theologians today. These themes are (1) true catholicity or varieties of inculturation within Catholic unity; (2) the question of women's role in the church

---

[26]See his article, "La littérature comme 'lieu' de la théologie," *Revue des sciences philosophiques et théologiques* 53 (1969) 70-80. See also several chapters describing similar aspects of twelfth-century theology in his study, so seminal for all medievalists, *La théologie au douzième siècle* (Paris: Vrin, 1957); the English translation by Jerome Taylor and Lester Little, *Nature, Man, and Society in the Twelfth Century* (Chicago: University of Chicago Press, 1968) unfortunately omits a number of important chapters.

and world, itself an outstanding example of the need for catholicity and inculturation; (3) the meeting of Christianity with the other great world religions (and, within this, the special problem of Christianity and Judaism); and (4) the ecumenical movement among Christians. In each of these fields the treasures preserved by the history of theology, treasures often to be regained and exploited, can make important contributions to theology. (I leave aside another very important area, issues in morality, since I have done less in that field, except for spirituality.)

(1) With respect to catholicity and inculturation, the history of theology can lead theologians to discern principles for inculturating the gospel. Examples that immediately come to mind are the inculturation of the Gospel in Greek and in Roman societies, and later in the societies of western Europe and of the Slavic peoples in eastern Europe. A more recent example is found in liberation theology. At an international meeting of theologians in Brussels in 1970, sponsored by *Concilium,* I heard Gustavo Gutiérrez state that the theology of this meeting had relied too much on past European theology for its problems and categories of inquiry; he said that something new would have to be launched and worked out for South America. And so he went back and further developed the theology of liberation he had already sketched for the bishops of CELAM at Medellin.[27] More recently still, Juan Luis Segundo has looked to principles of inculturation to understand what he calls a shift in or a second phase of liberation theology, one that is even more inculturated and less dependent on European concepts.[28]

In the past, on the other hand, most missionaries and theologians, ignoring past diversities and examples of inculturation, simply exported a western brand of Christianity everywhere or resisted attempts at inculturation. I saw this on my visits in China, and one has only to recall the curial rejection of Matteo Ricci's attempts at inculturation in China. Then there are the examples of the native peoples of North and South America (where, however, the Jesuit missionaries quite exceptionally tried to achieve a true inculturation of the Gospel among the various peoples they served), of the aborigines of Australia, of the peoples of Africa and Brazil, where modern syncretist religions show that Christianity has not taken full cultural roots. Here in Toronto, as in many larger North American cities, immigration has introduced an amazing variety of cultures all jostling together; theologians must help pastors to understand the need for varieties of inculturation even within one city. Past history and theology were not known sufficiently to give principles or guidance for undertaking inculturation, including the necessary critique of cultural traditions opposed to the Gospel but also the enriching of Chris-

---

[27]His first major work on this theme, *Teología de la liberación,* appeared in 1971. He had made his first sketch of this theology in 1968, he says in an interview he gave in late 1983 or early 1984; for the interview see *La Documentation Catholique,* no. 1881 (7 octobre 1984) 906-909.

[28]See an interview published ibid. 912-17, as well as his Toronto lecture, *The Shift within Latin American Theology* (Toronto: Regis College, 1962), and chapter 4 of his book, *Theology and the Vatican: A Response to Cardinal Ratzinger and a Warning to the Whole Church,* trans. John W. Diercksmeier (New York: Winston Press, A Seabury Book; London: Geoffrey Chapman, 1985).

tianity by the gospel's coming alive in these new cultures. Today our scriptural and patristic scholars have shown us the diversity that existed in the early church; historical studies have made us more aware of Near Eastern varieties of Christianity, as in Syria, Lebanon, Ethiopia, and Coptic Egypt; we have learned about movements by missionaries to China attempting a synthesis between Christian and Buddhist thought.[29] All these and other historical research can shed light on the need for a variety of theologies and, yes, of catechisms and liturgies related to different cultures.

The very history of the notion of true catholicity could also contribute. The early Fathers were astounded by the fact that such a variety of peoples and cultures could be one in fundamental faith. I have attempted a brief sketch of the application of different notions of catholicity historically in relation to local cultural identities.[30] A thorough history of the interpretation of this theme and of how it has been applied would be a fruitful kind of study.

(2) With respect to the theology of women, we can see the history of theology becoming a launching pad for new theological insights if we look at how much scholars in this field are having recourse to historical studies—biblical, patristic, medieval, and modern. These historical studies help us to discern how we got where we are, and to understand developments that are not only contingent historically but also destructive of gospel values. Although some of this research needs to be critiqued,[31] much of it is exceptionally good and is raising fundamental questions for all theology.[32] Although some in this area of research might say that history is bunk and that we simply have to begin afresh, unfettered by the past, these his-

---

[29]A doctoral thesis at St. Michael's by John Kasserow of the Maryknoll Missionaries has studied this attempt at inculturation; he bases his work on both written documents and artistic remains.

[30]This was done in a paper read at the International History of Religions Conference in Sydney, Australia, in 1986, whose theme was "Identity Issues and World Religions." The paper was entitled: "Catholicity: A Threat or a Help to Identity?" It examined how the interpretation of catholicity has varied from unity within variety to uniformity and how these and other interpretations have affected different cultural situations and identities.

[31]One influential example that a group of us read and discussed is the work, interesting and valuable for its historical data but quite unilateral and tendentious, of Marina Warner, *Alone of All Her Sex: The Myth and the Cult of the Virgin Mary* (New York: Knopf, 1976). A great deal of good scholarship cannot hide the bias, narrowness, and unfounded sweeping generalizations of the work. Warner ignores or denies the beneficial role of Marian devotion, despite its evident aberrations, in overcoming exclusively masculine symbolization of God, the role of popular religious practice in the pastoral field, or the profound psychological import of a benevolent female intercessor. Her introduction seems to reveal the reason for her bias in seeing Marian devotion almost exclusively as a source of guilt for those who do not measure up to Mary.

[32]For example, Elizabeth Schüssler Fiorenza, *In Memory of Her* (New York: Crossroad, 1984); Elizabeth Gussmann's studies and editing of a series of volumes of texts in her *Archiv für philosophie- und theologiegeschichtliche Frauenforschung* (Munich: Iudicium, 1984 ff.); Joanne Wolski Conn, ed., *Women's Spirituality: Resources for Christian Develoment* (New York: Paulist Press, 1986); Anne Carr, *Transforming Grace: Christian Traditions and Women's Experience* (San Francisco: Harper and Row, 1988).

torical studies of theology in various cultural contexts are proving to be a liberating and stimulating launching pad. Thus, for example, every conference on medieval thought or culture has several papers or even several sessions recovering the important thought and role of women. The intellectual, artistic, and spiritual importance of medieval women such as Hrostvitha von Gandersheim, Hildegard of Bingen, Heloise, Julian of Norwich, Catherine of Siena and many others is being highlighted, and this includes their contributions to theology as well as to the culture in which theology developed.[33]

(3) For the meeting of Christianity with other religions there is perhaps less in the way of positive good to be found in the history of our theology since until recently so much of it negated the value of other religions. Yet two points come to mind: (a) I remember Canon Moeller of Belgium describing how, in preparing documents on non-Christian religions for the Second Vatican Council, the drafters appealed to the teaching of some of the Fathers about the Word's constantly coming into the world, to pagans as well as to Christians; (b) The history of the doctrine that outside the church there is no salvation and the changing interpretation of this doctrine through history (not yet fully researched), is an extraordinary example of how past theology, meeting with new human and Christian experiences, can set theologians off in new directions.

(4) As for the ecumenical movement, anyone who has participated in ecumenical study and dialogue knows how much the history of theology has contributed to dissipating incorrect judgments about others, to mutual understanding, to finding common grounds of agreement. How could the various agreed statements (ARCIC, Catholic-Lutheran, BEM) have come about without the presence and contribution of theologians fully acquainted with the history of theologies concerning ministry, authority, the sacraments, justification, and other basic problems of the churches?

Moreover, the present agenda of the Faith and Order Commission of the World Council of Churches invites the churches to a common expression of apostolic faith today; this is being done by taking as the basic reference point the Nicene-Constantinople Creed. Meetings based on this creed have already been held with respect to creation and to confessing Christ crucified in our social, cultural and ethical settings; others this year and next will examine ecclesiology and pneumatology. The evocation of so historically situated a creed as this for a test of apostolic faith clearly indicates the role that the history of theology will play in these years preparatory to the next General Assembly of the World Council in Canberra in 1991.

An example here in Canada is an official dialogue between Catholics and the United Church of Canada (which grew out of Congregationalist, Methodists, and some Presbyterians); of late we have been examining the notion of authority in the two traditions and therefore studying the papacy. It was very instructive to bring

---

[33]For brief accounts of these medieval women see, among others, Sandro Sticca, "Hrostvitha," *Dictionary of the Middle Ages* 6 (1985) 313-16; Ernst H. Soudex, "Hildegard of Bingen," ibid. 228-29; Valerie M. Lagorio, "Julian of Norwich," ibid. 7 (1986) 179-80; "Abelard, Peter," ibid. 1 (1982) 16-20; (Heloise is considered only under Abelard!). For Catherine of Siena, curiously neglected in this dictionary, see other encyclopedias.

into the discussions the history of how the theology of the papacy developed over the centuries. Especially valuable was the historical re-examination of the true teaching of the First Vatican Council over against the exaggerated interpretations that have often prevailed since then. As one example, the statement that the pope is infallible of himself and not by the consent of the church has been shown to have been directed against a Gallican juridical requisition and not against the need for the pope to be in intimate contact with the faith of the whole church. This historical clarification has opened the way for developing the theology of consensus of the faithful and of reception. (Here, by the way, is an immense field of historical research that should be illuminating—the history of how reception has taken place in the past and what was and what was not received. Margaret O'Gara's recent book on the attitude of the French minority at Vatican I can serve as an example of illuminating historical research that can help contemporary theology.)[34]

With respect to ecumenicity and ecclesiology in general, historical research opens four areas that have been neglected too long: (a) The application of contextual historical hermeneutics to Catholic conciliar statements and definitions. These are time-conditioned statements and must be understood in their context and in relation to the precise question being asked. Historical studies of past conciliar statements can also lead to a better understanding of the restricted meaning given by earlier councils to terms such as "faith," "heresy," and "anathema." Examination of this hermeneutical question grew significantly in the late sixties and early seventies;[35] (b) The question whether the general councils held in the West since the split between the Eastern and Western Churches are truly ecumenical or are only general synods of the West: the 2nd Vatican Council's recognition of the Orthodox as "Church" raises this question about western councils (those of the Lateran, Lyons, Vienne, Constance, Florence, Trent, Vatican), in which the Or-

---

[34]It is entitled *Triumph in Defeat: Infallibility, Vatican I, and the French Minority Bishops* (Washington, D.C.: Catholic University of America Press, 1988).

[35]See my article, "The Hermeneutic of Roman Catholic Dogmatic Statements," *SR: Studies in Religion/Sciences Religieuses* 2 (1972) 157-75, which includes references to a number of pioneering articles of the late sixties and early seventies by Albert Lang, Piet Fransen, Piet Schoonenberg, Karl Rahner, E. Schillebeeckx, Gregory Baum, Avery Dulles and others. One important result of Lang's historical studies is to see that councils prior to Vatican I used the terms "faith," "heresy," and "anathema" in a broader, less precisely defined sense than that of Vatican I. These referred primarily to separation from the unity of the church because of persistent disobedience to the church, but did not mean that the teachings being upheld against those proclaimed heretics or anathema were divinely revealed truths. Yet this is what most unhistorically trained theologians have held when assigning "theological notes" to various propositions. See Albert Lang, "Der Bedeutungswandel der Befriffe 'fides' und 'haeresis' und die dogmatische Wertung der Konzilsentscheidungen von Vienne und Trient," *Münchener Theologische Zeitschrift* 4 (1953) 133-46. See also Piet Fransen, "Réflexions sur l'anathème au Concile de Trente . . . , " *Ephemerides Theologicae Louvanienses* 29 (1953) 659-72; idem, "The Authority of the Councils," in John M. Todd, ed., *Problems of Authority* (Baltimore: Helicon, 1962), 43-78; and idem, "Einige Bemerkungen zu den theologischen Qualifikationen," in Piet Schoonenberg, ed., *Die Interpretation des Dogmas,* trans. H. A. Mertens (Düsseldorf: Patmos, 1969) 111-37.

thodox did not participate;[36] (c) The hierarchy of truths, indicated long ago by Thomas Aquinas[37] and stated clearly in the context of ecumenism by Vatican II, opens up important possibilities for dialogue among the churches. Once again historical studies can help to clarify not only this notion but also the content of this hierarchy.[38] (d) The recognition by Vatican II of the distinctive theological elaborations of doctrines by the traditions of the Orthodox and the West, as well as appreciation of their distinctive liturgies, spiritualities, and canonical traditions, also invites historical investigation that can give new insights and possibilities to theologians.[39] These are four issues that, I think, will launch us into blue-sky thinking that may be unsettling for some but liberating and hopeful for others.

In ecclesiology, the history of theology can also illumine the current discussion about the theological character of episcopal conferences. The theology of the historical patriarchs and their synods, of the role and doctrinal contributions of regional and local councils, and the history of the development of various organs of local or national church government, can help perspectives on this issue, which to many looks a like an assertion of curial power against episcopal bodies. In this struggle there have been several statements to episcopal conferences by Pope John Paul II in which he seems to have distanced himself from some of his curial officials.[40]

---

[36]Yves Congar, Jean-Marie Tillard and others have raised this question; they seem to think that even if the councils since Second Nicea (or perhaps even since Chalcedon) are not truly ecumenical and have not been received by the Orthodox or by other Christians, they still represent a generally valid teaching by and for one broad section of the church, much as did local, regional, or national synods in the past. Some of them suggest that church union might be envisaged without requiring the other churches to accept the teachings of these western councils. Luis M. Bermejo's book of essays, *Towards Christian Reunion: Vatican I: Obstacles and Opportunities* (Gujaharat Sahitya Prakash, Anand, Gujarat, 388 001, India, 1984), is more radical. Vatican II's recognition of the Orthodox as Church and of Anglicans and Protestant bodies as ecclesial communities means for him that Vatican I's definition of infallibility of papal teaching and of universal jurisdiction has no claim to ecumenical conciliar authority.

[37]See *Summa theologiae* II-II, q. 1, aa. 6-10, on the articles of faith.

[38]See *Decretum de oecumenismo*, 11; in *Conciliorum oecumenicorum decreta*, 3rd ed., ed. G. Alberigo et al. (Bologna, 1973) 915: "Insuper in dialogo oecumenico theologi catholici . . . una cum fratribus seiunctis investigationem peragentes de divinis mysteriis . . . meminerint [in comparandis doctrinis] existere ordinem seu 'hierachiam' veritatum doctrinae catholicae, cum diversus sit earum nexus cum fundamento fidei christianae."

[39]See ibid. 15-17; ed. Alberigo, 916-19. Note no. 17 (p. 919): "Quae supra de legitima diversitate dicta sunt, eadem placet etiam de diversa theologica doctrinarum enuntiatione declarare. Etenim in veritatis revelatae exploratione methodi gressusque diversi ad divina cognoscenda et confitenda in Oriente et in Occidente adhibiti sunt. Unde mirum non est quosdam aspectus mysterii revelati quandoque magis congrue percipi et in meliorem lucem poni ab uno quam ab altero, ita ut tunc variae illae theologicae formulae non raro potius inter se compleri dicendae sint quam opponi." The Council goes on to point out special valuable characteristics of Eastern theological traditions.

[40]My private study done for the Canadian Episcopal Conference (7 March 1987) contains many texts of John Paul II stating the truly collegial character of episcopal conferences working with him. These are conveniently ignored by the preparatory document sent

I mentioned spirituality, and here as well the history of theology is an illuminating source for contemporary theological spirituality, that is, a spirituality that feeds, as I think it should, on the whole of theology. The history of theological spirituality is recovering many treasures from different Catholic traditions; at the same time, it cautions against a fundamentalist application of past authors and spiritualities to contemporary times: a hermeneutic of past authors and spiritualities is as essential as a hermeneutic of scripture, dogmatic definitions, or theol-

---

out by the Congregation for Bishops. Some but not all of the pope's statements have been collected by Adriano Garuti, *La collegialità oggi e domani* (Bologna: Edizioni Francescane Bologna, 1982). These statements were ignored as well as by the document issued by the International Theological Commission, *L'unique Église du Christ* (Paris: Le Centurion, 1985); Latin text: *Themata selecta de ecclesiologia occasione XX anniversarii conclusionis Concilii Oecumenici Vaticani II,* Documenta, 13 (Vatican City, 1985). It claims instead that episcopal collegiality belongs to the very structure of the church by divine right (*jure divino*), but that institutions such as episcopal conferences belong to the organization of the concrete figure of the church (*jure ecclesiastico*), and concludes that the use concerning these latter of terms such as "college," "collegiality," and "collegial" "ne peut donc relever que d'un sens *analogique, théologiquement impropre*" (p. 38: emphasis mine; Latin text, 34). To apply a distinction between what is of divine right and what is of ecclesiastical right in this case is highly questionable; even worse is the statement that terms used analogically are "theologically improper." This amounts to saying that all theology, which can only speak analogically about God and the divine mysteries, speaks "improperly"! The inconsistency of the document is shown by the fact that earlier, speaking about the theology of the Trinity, it says: "Nous pouvons appliquer analogiquement(!) ces réflexions à la théologie de l'Église" (p. 35; Latin text, 31). The commission could hardly mean that its analogical application to the church is to be taken as "théologiquement impropre"! The credibility of the phrase, "sens analogique, théologiquement impropre," as well as the whole teaching of the document at this point, is seriously weakened by the circumstances leading to its acceptance by the commission (it passed by a vote of only sixteen out of the twenty-seven who voted; the other nine either voted negatively or abstained); I was a member of the commission at the time, and this account is based on things recorded during the meeting. The whole paragraph containing this rejection of the proper collegiality of episcopal conferences was added to the earlier draft of the text by the sub-commission preparing the document and was given to the members only as they gathered for its meeting. This final draft was put to a vote without the members being allowed to discuss the change and without the usual procedure of voting chapter by chapter. This unusual procedural decision was made by a majority (only) of the sub-commission and was approved by Cardinal Ratzinger, the president of the commission; this represented a conflict of interest on his part because the opinion added to the text is that of Cardinal Ratzinger himself. (I regard this account as no violation of confidence since such procedures have no right to protection from exposure; the church needs criticism of these kinds of activities.) Further criticism of the document by John Thornhill (also a member of the commission at the time) in "The Church and the Churches," *The Tablet* (23 November 1985) 1242-43. The phrase in question was quoted, but then contradicted twice, in the preliminary document on episcopal conferences sent out by the Congregation for Bishops (12 January 1988). For judgments on this document see Avery Dulles, "What is the Role of a Bishops' Conference?" *Origins* 17, no. 46 (28 April 1968) 789, 791-96; idem, "The Mandate to Teach," *America* (19 March 1988) 293-95; James H. Provost, "Questions of Communion and Credibility," ibid. 296-98; Ladislas Orsy, "Some Questions from History," ibid. 299-301; Joseph A. Komonchak, "Bishops Conferences and Collegiality," ibid. 302-304.

ogies of the past. One has to reckon, for instance, with the Platonism and/or Stoicism found in many of the Fathers to see possible elements of distortion in their spirituality. In the middle ages, the theme of *contemptus mundi* influenced many monastic spiritualities and is hardly a good guide for lay persons living in the world.[41]

I was originally asked to speak in this paper about medieval theologians, and especially Thomas Aquinas, as sources of theology, and I would like to say at least a few words about this. Earlier I mentioned Chenu's contribution in calling attention to the importance of symbolism, literature, and the rest for theological method. I remember asking him one time in the early 1950's, as I was somewhat overwhelmed by the new biblical, patristic, and contemporary movements in theology in Paris, what was the point of studying medieval theology, including Thomas Aquinas. His reply was that the medieval scholastics, while limited in many ways, can teach us a certain rigor and discipline in theology, a rigor and discipline that might sometimes be less operative today as theologians try new methods in their research. Moreover, theologians such as Albert the Great and Thomas Aquinas, by daring to use newly-acquired philosophies and natural sciences within faith, challenge us to do in our day what they did in theirs with respect to the new resources at our disposal.

Again, although the practice of medieval theologians of making distinctions no longer appeals to moderns, at least in its later exaggerated forms, the moderate use of distinctions by the great medieval theologians can show us how we can absorb into a synthesis those aspects of an opposed position that are congenial with our own; making distinctions can also allow various elements of a problem to be given their respective due: "distinguish in order to unite" according to Jacques Maritain's phrase.[42]

There are also some fundamental insights not only in great patristic authors such as Origen, Basil, the Gregories, or Augustine, but also in theologians like Aquinas, Bonaventure, Albert, Duns Scotus and others—insights that can continue to nourish contemporary theologians, or at least remind or even challenge them in their research. The day is long past, thank God, when it was enough to settle a theological discussion to say: "St. Augustine says," "St. Thomas says" (or for Franciscans, "Scotus" or "Bonaventure" or perhaps "Ockham says").

---

[41]On how to study spirituality see my article, "Toward Defining Spirituality," *SR: Studies in Religion/Sciences Religieuses* 12 (1983) 127-41, and the brochure, *Thomas Aquinas' Spirituality,* The Étienne Gilson Series, 7 (Toronto: Pontifical Institute of Mediaeval Studies, 1984).

[42]This is part of the title of one his most famous books, *Distinguer pour unir, ou Les degrés du savoir,* 2nd ed. (Paris: Desclée de Brouwer, 1946). See the Préface: " 'Personne, dit Tauler, n'entend mieux la vraie distinction que ceux qui sont entrs dans l'unité; et de même personne ne connaît vraiment l'unité s'il ne connait aussi la distinction. Tout effort de synthèse métaphysique, particulièrement s'il porte sur les complexes richesses de la connaissance et de l'esprit, doit donc distinguer pour unir." See also M.-D. Chenu, *Toward Understanding St. Thomas,* trans. A.-M. Landry and D. Hughes (Chicago: Regnery, 1964) 173-76; French original: *Introduction à l'étude de S. Thomas d'Aquin* (Montréal-Paris, 1954; rpt. 1972) 146-50.

But who can doubt that these great theologians merit continuing historical study? If you look at the offerings in philosophy in any worthwhile university department of philosophy, at least on the graduate level, you will always find courses in Aristotle, Plato, Plotinus, Descartes, Kant, Hume, Locke, Leibniz, Spinoza, Hegel, Husserl, etc.—and here at Toronto, because of St. Michael's College and our Institute, medieval thinkers are well represented in philosophy as well. These are not taken as last-word authorities, but as great moments in the history of philosophy; they have set the course of so much later philosophy; without them we cannot understand contemporary thought; they continue to provide insight and inspiration without their being repeated uncritically. To meet a great mind of the present or past is one of the most important things any student or scholar can do—this is true for the history of theology, especially study of texts of the great classics. The work of David Tracy on the importance of classics, and the questions of interpretation involved in reading them, naturally come to mind here.[43]

How, I ask, can a serious school or department of Catholic theology allow students to proceed to doctorates without requiring them to know at least some of the classics of the patristic, medieval, or earlier modern period of Catholic theology? Among those reviewing theological education, there is a growing concern about the tendency of young research scholars to ignore the great figures of the past and to work only in contemporary theologians; the work of these contemporary theologians may be exciting for the moment but their durability and even the lasting value of their problematic is far from proven. Study of the history of theology shows the relativity of particular periods and views—and is thus a warning to ourselves not to take our own period as the final and best answer.

If I may spend a moment on Thomas Aquinas, I would like to point out a few areas where I think he can contribute to contemporary theology.

—He was a scriptural theologian all his life—his main teaching was his continual commenting on scripture; his example, and the richness of his commentaries, can urge us always to remain in close contact with the biblical sources of our theology.

—He is constantly aware of mystery. Thus he says we know more *quomodo Deus NON sit* than *quomodo Deus sit;* he is always aware of the inadequacy of our analogical terms. When he uses created concepts analogically, he so frequently makes what I call "mental genuflections," prefixing the terms with *quidam, quaedam, quoddam, quasi* to indicate their inadequacy to the mystery. For example, for him Christ's humanity is "quoddam instrumentum," "a kind of instrument," and when he speaks about Christ's saving us by way of *redemption,* he says that Christ's blood, was "quasi quoddam pretium"—"as it were, a kind of price"! Would that modern theologians were always so aware of the inadequacy of the terms we use about the mysteries. How often we take analogies as adequate to the mystery!

—His original theology of *esse* or the *actus essendi,* together with themes of participation by creatures in divine *esse,* which allow him to account for a con-

---

[43]See his recent work *Plurality and Ambiguity: Hermeneutics, Religion, Hope* (San Francisco: Harper and Row, 1987).

tinuing presence of God in the deepest level of our being even while God transcends us infinitely.

—His theology of the missions and indwelling of the Trinitarian persons, showing the link of the inner life of God with salvation-history; this is one indication of how fully historical and personalist Thomas is, despite frequent misjudgments.[44]

—His theology of creation. Thomas gives natures their due; he has respect for intrinsic finalities of creatures. This makes his theology a source of a spirituality for laity in the world. This, however, is not the so-called "creation-centered spirituality" of Matthew Fox; Aquinas' theological spirituality is God-originating and God-oriented, but it does, within that orientation, respect the good of creatures and their development to their full potential.[45]

—His theology of diversity within creation and within the order of grace, this diversity giving greater glory to God than if there were none. This is a basis for ecological theology, for respect for every degree of being and respect for each person; it is an explanation of the variety of gifts, graces, and charisms in the church.

—The human person as the image of God and the Trinity, as the key to personal development spiritually; as the basis of moral prudential judgment, for, like God, the human intellectual agent is a free actor and decision-maker. This yields a morals of intrinsic values, not of obligation or external command.

— His theology of the New Law of Christian freedom, which has been praised by S. Lyonnet as a faithful recovery for the West of Paul's doctrine.[46] For Thomas the New Law is the grace of the indwelling Holy Spirit; written laws, commands, etc., are secondary, educative, and dispositive, and could, if made primary, be deadly.

—Thomas' stress on prudence and self-counselling rather than on unthinking obedience to superiors, directors, etc., obedience being required in relation to the common good and not simply to the will of the superior as such.

—The way Thomas integrates the emotions or passions in moral life, not their suppression as in so much Christian spirituality of the will. The role of the virtues of temperance and fortitude in ordering, from within the sensitive appetites, the passions or emotions. Christ as the supreme example of this.

---

[44]Max Seckler, in the introduction to his *Das Heil in der Geschichte: Geschichtstheologisches Denken bei Thomas von Aquin* (Munich, 1964), tells how he started his research by looking to Thomas Aquinas as a foil to later more history-linked theology, only to find that Aquinas is so historical in his theology that Seckler devoted his entire Habilitationsschrift to Thomas' doctrine. French translation of his work: *Le Salut et l'histoire: La pensée de saint Thomas d'Aquin sur la théologie de l'histoire,* Cogitatio fidei, 21 (Paris, 1967).

[45]See Chenu, *St Thomas d'Aquin et la théologie,* Maîtres spirituels, no. 17 (Paris: Seuil, 1960), or my essay, *Thomas Aquinas' Spirituality,* The Étienne Gilson Lecture, 1984, The Étienne Gilson Series, 7 (Toronto: Pontifical Institute of Mediaeval Studies, 1984).

[46]"St. Paul: Liberty and Law," in *The Bridge: A Yearbook of Judaeo-Christian Studies* IV, ed. John M. Oesterreicher (New York: Pantheon, 1962) 229-51.

—The instrumental role of Christ's humanity. By this approach Thomas integrates the whole theology of Christ's life—and especially his resurrection together with the passion and death—in ways that recapture the Pauline theology.

—His theology of sacramental sign and causality by signification, the basis for some in their work in the liturgical renewal.

—His theology of the church. The centrality of Christ's Headship by grace and of the Holy Spirit as the Heart of the church, the one identical person of the Holy Spirit giving the most fundamental unity to the church.

— His notion of catholicity based on his doctrine of the role of diversity in creation and in grace.

—His theology of faith, which integrates intellectual and affective aspects in the act of faith. For him the act of faith goes beyond and through propositions to the very reality of the mystery of God. This gives a solid basis for understanding the development of dogma and for relativizing propositions about the mysteries of faith.

—His theology of charity as friendship with God, and the overflow of intense union with God by love into a contemplative mystical knowledge by connaturality.[47]

Conclusion

From all that I have said, I think you can see my answer to the question in the title. The history of theology can be and has been used badly as a source of theology, but it can also be a good source as a fortress preserving the treasures of the past to be used with probity, with "cool ecstasy" in the present; it can thus serve as a launching pad sending theologians into new spheres of research and insight. There are many other launching pads today —sciences such as psychology, sociology, semiotics, and linguistics; methods such as narrative or praxis; new philosophies to use within faith. I would suggest that we construct one of these launching pads within the courtyard of the fortress of the history of theology. Using the past as a launching pad for creative theologies in the present and future will prevent a stagnating fortress use of past theology and at the same time (to change the metaphor) provide a gravitational pull that will keep space-travelling theologians from floating off into the darkness of outer space.

Finally, I would invite you to look at the history of theology within the history of salvation. God's saving grace comes to individuals and to the whole human community within history.[48] Part of that saving grace is surely the communication and reception of the Word of God, and this takes place in history; therefore, theo-

---

[47]Some of these items have been dealt with in the essay on Thomas Aquinas' theological spirituality indicated above, n. 45. Others will be presented in an essay to be published in *Spiritualities of the Heart,* ed. Annice Callahan (New York: Paulist Press, 1989 [at the press]), entitled: "Affectivity and the Heart in Thomas Aquinas' Spirituality."

[48]See the stimulating chapter, "The History of Salvation and Revelation," in Karl Rahner, *Foundations of Christian Faith,* trans. William V. Dych (New York: Seabury, 1978) 138-75.

logical reflection on the Word of God and on the Christian community's experience of this Word also takes place in history. (I try to emphasize this especially to students preparing for either lay or ordained ministry, especially at the beginning and end of a course of theology. For this particular group, to be studying theology together in preparation for ministering the Word of God to people of this time and many places is itself an important moment in salvation-history for today and for the moments of history in which they will minister.) To ignore the history of theology would be to cut oneself off from an aspect of salvation-history itself that has been and is important for the Christian community.[49] In the liturgy we engage in thankful eucharistic *anamnesis* of God's wondrous saving works; so we theologians should engage in thankful *anamnesis* of God's saving activity on our behalf, that is, God's saving activity of calling and aiding theologians in the ministry of research and teaching in order to bring God's saving word to God's people in each generation and culture. Our joyful if sometimes difficult ministry and service involves us in using the history of theology as both a good fortress activity and a good launching pad. To put it differently, here in Canada we have a political party whose name, if not its policies, might express it in another way: theologians must be progressive conservatives, or perhaps conservative progressives. But Jesus put it best: we should hope to be scribes "trained for" (RSV) or "instructed in" (TOB)) the kingdom of heaven, so as to be like the wise householder, who brings forth from the household treasure *kaina kai palaia:* "what is new and what is old."

WALTER H. PRINCIPE, C.S.B.
Pontifical Institute of Mediaeval Studies, Toronto

---

[49]On this, see the recent posthumous essay by Karl Rahner, "Dogmengeschichte in meiner Theologie," in *Dogmengeschichte* (see above, n. 4) 324-25.

A RESPONSE TO WALTER PRINCIPE

It is a very great honor for me to be asked to respond to Father Principe's remarks and my greatest difficulty in doing so is that I wonder if he has really left
anything to be said on this subject. However, when he sent me his paper, he did
point out to me that he had done very little in the field of *moral* theology, and he
kindly suggested that since that is my area, I might want to extend and supplement
what he has to say and to develop my questions and criticisms out of that field. I
am going to follow the lead that he has suggested, offering a few supplementary
comments of my own from the field of moral theology, although certainly I would
never try to match Father Principe's breadth of learning in this or any other area.
Then I am going to raise one question that seems to me to arise both from Father
Principe's remarks and from what I'm going to say briefly now.

It might seem surprising at first to turn to the field of the history of moral theology as one more illustration of the irreducible historicity of all theological reflection. After all, it would seem that in moral theology, if anywhere, we are faced
with genuinely new questions generated by the unprecedented social circumstances and the new technologies of our age. And to some extent that intuition is
accurate. After all, I have found it frustratingly difficult to find much in Aquinas,
for example, that speaks directly to the issues surrounding genetic engineering, or
nuclear deterrence. (Inconsiderate of him!) Nonetheless, I would claim that in the
field of moral theology, too, we do find examples of the irreducible historicity of
theological reflection of which Father Principe speaks. For it must be noted that
the new circumstances and the new technological possibilities of our age, about
which we moral theologians exercise ourselves, do not generate moral quandaries
all by themselves. That is to say, we would not be facing the particular new questions that we do today if we had not already brought a particular set of convictions
and concerns to what is new in our situation. To take one admittedly not-so- new
example, abortion would not be the kind of issue that it is for us, it would not raise
the *particular* moral questions and dilemmas that it does, if we did not bring to
this issue a complex set of commitments both to individual autonomy and also to
equality. Or to take another, perhaps fresher, example, genetic engineering would
not raise the particular questions that it does for us if we did not come to it with
both a commitment to a certain veneration for nature and, once again, a respect
for individual freedom. Examples such as these have convinced me that in my field
as in all others we can never draw the line between past wisdom and present dilemmas too neatly. Rather, we find ourselves constantly in the midst of a living
tradition of belief, value, and thought that is defined as much by its recurring
problematics as by the substantive positions that we find its expositors taking.
Certainly, new questions arise within this tradition, particularly in its moral dimension. Nonetheless, even these new questions are fully significant and intelli-

gible for us only when we can see them as new instantiations, as it were, of the problematics which have structured our shared tradition from the beginning. And our attempts to resolve these questions will require us, at least at some points, to engage past attempts to resolve other expressions of the same recurring problematics.

Now all this is very well, but it does raise one critical question that Father Principe touches upon but does not develop and that I would like to sharpen now. And that is the question or the problem that is expressed, depending upon the circles in which you move, as the problem of historicism, the problem of the hermeneutical circle, the problem of relativism, or, in my field, the problem of sectarianism. Indeed, I have noticed a certain lack of the meeting of the minds between systematic theologians and moral theologians precisely on this question. In my experience, systematic theologians seem to me to be very comfortable with a general idea of the historicity of the theological tradition and the need to view the theological tradition in terms of its own particular, and in some ways very idiosyncratic developments. Moral theologians, on the other hand, while they recognize that to some extent this must be taken into account, nonetheless remain committed to the autonomy of morality from all particular traditions and ways of life, and therefore to the genuine possibility of establishing a universally valid moral law. And this, by the way, is true of moral theologians at all ends of the spectrum of the debates that are so much a part of moral theology today. When one comes across an ethicist who does want to take the particularity of the Christian moral tradition seriously, perhaps make it the foundation of his or her work, the cries of sectarianism go up to high heaven, and sometimes, fairly so. Nonetheless, this situation reflects the fact that there is a certain, shall we say, talking at cross purposes between systematic and moral theologians precisely in this area. Now this is a question that I feel with all the greater difficulty because I am convinced, like most of my colleagues in moral theology, that one cannot simply remain at the level of a particular moral tradition. That, it seems to me, is an inadequate way to deal with the very serious problems of moral pluralism and historicism. But while saying very clearly that I want to get out of the hermeneutical circle, I do want to raise the caution that to do so is by no means easy.

Let me point out first of all that the ability to raise questions within a tradition does not get us to the central problem. After all, everyone admits that we can raise questions within the particular moral and intellectual traditions that we inhabit; the issue is whether we can escape from the fundamental presuppositions and problematics that set those questions for us, or indeed, whether we should even *try* to escape from those fundamental presuppositions and problematics. Similarly, an examination of different historical positions, or even an examination of radically different religious and moral traditions can only serve to set the problem of historicism for us and to sharpen it. It cannot of and by itself provide us with a solution since the question is precisely whether we can choose among different historical and cultural options on the basis of anything other than sheer philosophical fiat.

These are the kinds of questions that any attempt to take seriously the history of theological and moral reflection must address at some point. And I can assure you that while I feel the force of the questions, while I feel it is critical to resolve them, I certainly would not attempt to give you any resolution of them here and now—I just want to sharpen the questions. I would say, however, that I have found resources for dealing with these problems that I might commend to you. Philosophically, I think the most recent work of Alasdair MacIntyre is extremely helpful in grappling with these issues.[1] Theologically, I think the work of Francis Fiorenza deserves special attention in this area.[2] Beyond that I have found it helpful to go back to the work of John Henry Newman, who in this, as in so many other areas, was anticipating the problems that trouble us more than a century before his time.[3]

JEAN PORTER
The Divinity School, Vanderbilt University

---

[1]Alasdair MacIntyre, *Whose Justice? Which Rationality* (South Bend IN: The University of Notre Dame Press, 1888).

[2]Francis Schussler Fiorenza, *Foundational Theology: Jesus and the Church* (New York: Crossroad Press, 1985).

[3]John Henry Newman, *An Essay on the Development of Christian Doctrine,* 16th ed. (London: Longmans, Green and Co., 1920).

EXPERIENCE AS A SOURCE FOR THEOLOGY

My task is to consider experience as a source for theology today. Of course experience has always functioned in theology although its function has not always been recognized. The question, according to Bernard Cooke, is not "*whether* experience is a basic source of theology but *how* we can accurately and critically use it."[1] The changing answer to this question lies at the heart of the contemporary transformation of theology.

This presentation has three parts: Part I will consider some shifts in how experience is being used as a source for theology today, with an emphasis on the foundational role of present experience and a recognition of the widening experiential base for theological reflection. Part II will consider aspects of my experience as a Canadian woman, focusing on three parallel transitions within the Canadian and the feminist context. Part III will suggest how my Canadian and feminist experiences may be used as a source for theology.

Before I begin it is necessary to clarify what I mean by experience. I am not using the term "experience" in a specialized philosophical way but in a common sense way. By experience I include all that contributes to our situation, both our political and personal context and our near and distant histories. Such an understanding of experience is open-ended and flexible rather than definitive. I speak of "religious experience," not in the restricted sense that William James used the term, as possessing an element which can be found nowhere else and which he defined as "the feelings, acts, and experiences of individual men [*sic*] in their solitude, so far as they apprehend themselves to stand in relation to whatever they may consider the divine."[2] Rather I am referring to what Rahner calls "transcendental experience," the human subject's orientation toward holy mystery which constitutes our essence as subject and as person.[3] In this sense all experience is "religious."

---

[1] Bernard Cooke, "The Experiential 'Word of God'," in Leonard Swidler, ed., *Consensus in Theology? A Dialogue with Hans Küng and Edward Schillebeeckx* (Philadelphia: Westminster Press, 1980) 72.

[2] William James, *The Varieties of Religious Experience: A Study in Human Nature,* Gifford Lectures on Natural Religion Delivered in Edinburgh 1901–1902 (London: Longmans, Green, & Co., 1935) 42. For a critique of William James' understanding of religious experience, see Nicholas Lash, *Easter in Ordinary: Reflections on Human Experience and the Knowledge of God* (Charlottesville: University Press of Virginia; London: SCM Press, 1988).

[3] Karl Rahner, *Foundations of Christian Faith: An Introduction to the Idea of Christianity* (New York: Crossroad, 1985), especially the Introduction and Chapters I and II. On p. 20 Rahner describes *transcendental experience* as "the subjective, unthematic, necessary and unfailing consciousness of the knowing subject that is co-present in every spiritual act of knowledge, and the subject's openness to the unlimited expanse of all possible reality."

Experience needs to be interpreted in order for us to make sense of it and to allow it to become shared experience. In our interpretation we use the language we have received, the stories we have been told. For Christians it is particularly the story of Jesus which provides meaning for our own story. Bringing together our experience and the Christian story is the task of Christian theology. Scripture and tradition are themselves codified collective human experience which we draw upon to illuminate our present experience.[4] There are significant shifts in the way that codified experience and present experience interact in theology. These shifts involve not only a change in method, but a change in the nature of theology itself.

I. SHIFTS IN THE USE OF EXPERIENCE AS SOURCE

Often the experience of the past, rather than the present, has been reflected upon by professional theologians, and then applied to contemporary situations. The newer use of experience in theology begins with communal contemporary experience and attempts to rediscover the tradition in light of this present experience. In the 1982 Marquette Theology Lecture Monika Hellwig described this process as "the real revolution in Christian theology."[5] Hellwig delineates two major strands in this shift in the very nature of theology. The first is the recovery of present experience in its full social and political dimensions as foundational for theology. The second is the concern to correct the bias in the experience which plays a foundational role in theology. Her question, one which challenges all of us, is "Whose experience counts in theological reflection?"

Focus on Present Experience. The roots of this emphasis on present experience may be found in earlier writers. One might think of George Tyrrell or Friedrich von Hügel, or of Vatican II's call to consider the "signs of the times." Rahner taught the Catholic theological world to recognize God's self-communication within the ordinary experience of ordinary people so that any authentic experience of self may be interpreted as an experience of God.[6] The implications of Rahner's insight about human experience as ground for theology are being worked out by many others. Anne Carr, writing in 1973, saw his work as "the bridge or transition between the old in Catholic thought and the yet unformed new."[7] In the past fifteen years that new has been taking shape.

Rahner's student, Johannes Baptist Metz, criticizes Rahner's transcendent theology as idealistic, individualistic, and ahistorical, arguing for a narrative and practical Christianity which takes more seriously the concrete historical and social

---

[4]Rosemary Radford Ruether makes this point in *Sexism and God-Talk: Toward a Feminist Theology* (Boston: Beacon Press, 1983) 12.

[5]Monika Hellwig, *Whose Experience Counts in Theological Reflection?* (Milwaukee: Marquette University Press, 1982) 6.

[6]Rahner, *Foundations* 126-33; "Reflections on the Experience of Grace," *Theological Investigations* 3 (London: Darton, Longman & Todd, 1967) 86-90.

[7]Anne Carr, "Theology and Experience in the Thought of Karl Rahner," *Journal of Religion* 53 (1973) 376.

situation in which subjects are placed.[8] He sees himself as continuing the work of his teacher by critiqueing and correcting it, just as Rahner had critiqued and corrected neoscholasticism.[9] This work of correction continues as theologians explore the complexities of contemporary experience and the focus shifts from the experience of individuals to the experience of communities.

The recovery of present experience as foundation for theology does not mean that the past is ignored, but rather that the past is appropriated by the present community in the light of present experience. James Dunn and James Mackey in their collaborative work, *New Testament Theology in Dialogue,* refer to the "merging of horizons of past and present."

> Most positively the point has been put that the past can only emerge at all for us, and the present can only come explicitly to consciousness, in the course of what has been called the merging of horizons of past and present, as we come with all the presuppositions of contemporary culture to a set of documents which, we must keep reminding ourselves, survive from an entirely different age.[10]

The task of hermeneutics is to bring together these horizons of past and present. But even in this merging the focus is on the present community which interprets the stories of the past in the light of its present concerns.

The Correction of Bias. I turn to the second shift in the use of experience as a source of theology: the correction of bias. Experiences previously ignored are becoming a source for theological reflection. The process is facilitated as the theological task is undertaken by women as well as men, by lay people as well as clerics, by communities as well as individuals. As persons and communities previously overlooked or externally defined reflect on their experiences of particularity, theology is being transformed.

The correction of bias includes a recognition that no theology can claim universality, that all theologies are political, shaped by their own context, and that this is true not only for contemporary theologies but for the theologies found in the Bible, in the great works of the early Christian and medieval theologians, and in the statements of the hierarchical magisterium.

Traditional Western theology is now seen as determined by dominant world powers and groups. The critique of this theology comes from the "new theologies" which argue that Western theology is culture bound, church-centered, male-dominated, age-dominated, procapitalist, anticommunist, nonrevolutionary, and overly theoretical.[11]

---

[8]Johannes Baptist Metz, *Faith in History and Society: Toward a Practical, Fundamental Theology,* tr. David Smith (London: Burns & Oates, 1980); first published in German as *Glaube in Geschichte und Gesellschaft* (Mainz: Matthias-Grunewald-Verlag, 1977). Matthew Lamb in *Solidarity with Victims: Toward a Theology of Social Transformation* (New York: Crossroad, 1982) 117-21 describes Metz's critique of Rahner's transcendental theology as "a dialectic of suspicion and recovery."

[9]Metz, *Faith in History and Society,* 11, n15.

[10]James D. G. Dunn and James P. Mackey, *New Testament Theology in Dialogue* (London: SPCK, 1987) 142.

[11]Tissa Balasuriya, an Asian theologian, makes this critique in *Planetary Theology* (London: SCM Press, 1984) 2-10.

Gutiérrez comments on the "new theologies":

> The theological schools that are growing up in the so-called Third World countries,
> or among the radically and culturally oppressed minorities of the wealthy nations,
> or in the context of women's liberation, are expressions of the new presence of those
> who have previously been "absent" from history. Their efforts spring from areas
> of humanity that have previously been arid, theologically speaking, but in which
> Christian faith has old and deep roots. Hence their present fruitfulness.[12]

As the literary critic, Elaine Showalter, points out: "In the past, female experience which could not be accommodated by androcentric models was treated
as deviant or simply ignored."[13] This happened to the experiences of other groups
who constitute a *muted group,* the boundaries of whose culture and reality overlap
with, but are not wholly contained by, the *dominant group.*[14] A rich source for theology lies in the experience of these muted groups. Observation from the outside
is not the same as a voice speaking from within.

The experience of women becomes a valuable source for theology—the experience of oppression in all its myriad forms, including experiences of sexual ha-
rassment and violence; the experience of being a daughter, a sister, a mother; the
experience of being a female body, with its own rhythm such as menstruation and
menopause; the experience of giving birth; the growing consciousness of sister-
hood with women everywhere. All of these experiences are recognized as a locus
of the divine and a source for theology. Likewise the experience of native peoples,
including their relationship to the land, their struggles to overcome internalized as
well as external oppression, and their efforts to reclaim their culture, becomes a
new source for theology.

However, it is not simply a matter of adding the experiences of those who have
been previously ignored. There is a need to correct what has been presented as
"human experience" by showing that the base for this experience is limited and
distorted. Feminist theorists argue for a new epistemology. The work of Sandra
Harding and Merrill Hintikka demonstrates the inadequacy of the experiential base
for all knowledge:

> What counts as knowledge must be grounded on experience. Human experience
> differs according to the kinds of activities and social relations in which humans en-
> gage. Women's experience systematically differs from the male experience on which
> the prevailing claims have been grounded. Thus the experience on which the pre-
> vailing claims to social and natural knowledge are founded is, first of all, only par-
> tial human experience only partially understood: namely, masculine experience as
> understood by men. However, when this experience is presumed to be gender-

---

[12]Gustavo Gutiérrez, "Speaking about God," in Geffré, Gutiérrez and Elizondo, eds.,
Different Theologies, Common Responsibility: Babel or Pentecost? Concilium 171 (Edinburgh: T.& T. Clark, 1984) 27.

[13]Elaine Showalter, "Feminist Criticism in the Wilderness," *Critical Inquiry* 8 (1981)
199.

[14]The categories of muted and dominant have been used by anthropologists to study
women in different societies. See Shirley Ardener, ed., *Perceiving Women* (London: Mal-
aby Press, 1975).

free—when the male experience is taken to be the human experience—the resulting theories, concepts, methodologies, inquiry goals and knowledge-claims distort human social life and human thought.[15]

Harding and Hintikka's analysis applies to theology as well as to philosophy and the social and natural sciences. It is necessary to identify how exclusively masculine perspectives on masculine experience have shaped systematic thought in theology and to identify aspects of women's experience which provide resources for a fuller understanding of human experience. This does not mean simply adding information about women to male categories of thought but critiquing the very categories themselves, our ways of knowing and the organization of society.

There is no universal human experience, nor is there any universal "women's experience." New knowledge which is becoming available through women's studies enables us to recognize the pluralism of women's experience across different cultures, races, and classes.[16] Problems of sexism are interstructured with racism and classism. Patterns and structures of patriarchy, domination. and exploitation are deeply engrained in all societies, and are evident in the home and church as well as in other institutions.[17]

In the past twenty years feminist theologians have begun to critique this patriarchal bias in theology. As Elisabeth Schüssler Fiorenza and others emphasize, "Sexism in theology is not so much a personal fault as a structural evil that distorts and corrupts theology and the Christian message."[18] If it is true that sexism does distort theology and the Christian message, it is crucial to study how this is so, and to begin the work of correction.

II. A CANADIAN AND FEMINIST PERSPECTIVE

In Part I, I considered two shifts in the way experience functions as a source in theology, the recovery of present experience and the correction of bias in the experience which is foundational for theology. In Part II, I will consider two forms that contemporary "corrective" theologies have taken: contextual theologies over

[15]Sandra Harding and Merrill Hintikka, eds., Introduction to *Discovering Reality: Feminist Perspectives on Epistemology, Metaphysics, Methodology, and Philosophy of Science* (Dordrecht, Holland: D. Reidel, 1983) x.

[16]As Sandra Harding notes: "Feminism has played an important role in showing that there are not now and never have been any generic 'men' at all—only gendered men and women. Once essential and universal man dissolves, so does his hidden companion, woman. We have, instead, myriads of women living in elaborate historical complexes of class, race, and culture." "The Instability of the Analytical Categories of Feminist Theory," *Signs: Journal of Women in Culture and Society* 2 (1986) 647.

[17]See Elisabeth Schüssler Fiorenza and Anne Carr, eds., *Women, Work and Poverty, Concilium* 194 (Edinburgh: T.&T. Clark, 1987) for a study of these patterns in different cultural situations.

[18]Elisabeth Schüssler Fiorenza, "Towards a Liberating and a Liberated Theology: Women Theologians and Feminist Theology in the USA," in Jossua and Metz, eds., *Doing Theology in New Places, Concilium* 115 (New York: Seabury, 1979) 27-28.

against a theology which claims to be universal but which in fact is conditioned by its own cultural context, and feminist theologies over against androcentric theologies.

I will consider how these "correctives" are shaping my theology as a Canadian Catholic woman. I know that my theology is influenced by the fact that I am a woman rather than a man, a single woman who is a member of a religious congregation rather than a married woman; a woman living during the closing decades of the twentieth century rather than at any other period in human history; a Catholic woman rather than a Protestant or Jewish woman but one who teaches theology in an ecumenical context; a woman from a middle-class background; Canadian rather than British, American, or Latin American; a Torontonian rather than a Quèbeçoise, a Maritimer, or a Western Canadian. Out of my particular contexts arise experiences which are a source for my theology, which in turn can impact your theology. The rest of this paper will reflect on these experiences as a source for theology.

Some Common Transitions. Some beginning points for Canadian contextual theologies are emerging.[19] I have selected from the Canadian experience three transitions which have shaped the Canadian context: from survival in the wilderness to the survival of the world; from colonial status to global responsibility; from maintaining French and English culture to the acceptance and affirmation of pluralism. Three parallel transitions emerge from feminist experience. Just as Canada has moved from survival in the wilderness to concern for global survival, feminists have reflected on the transition from the identification of women with nature to women's concern for ecology. As Canada has moved from colonial status to global responsibility, women are moving from a position of being dominated to one of mutual empowerment. Canada's progression from the maintenance of two distinct cultures to the affirmation of pluralism is paralleled by the feminist move from woman's special role to the recognition of many different women's voices. The experience of each of these transformations challenges our image of God, of humanity, and of church.

Survival. As Mary Jo Leddy observes, "Between the facts of our Canadian society and the theological reflection on them, we need the mediating images of poets and artists, the revealing stories of writers, to give us some decisive insight into our reality here."[20] Margaret Atwood, in her search for shapes and patterns that characterize Canadian literature, argues that survival is the unifying and informing symbol for Canada. This image is explicitly chosen in contrast to the fre-

---

[19]At the CTSA in 1986, Dan Donovan presented the "Canadian Story" as part of the "Historical Context of North American Theology." Donovan ended his presentation by stating that "what is required at the moment is a greater sensitivity to the Canadian scene and to the need for an indigenous theology." *Catholic Theological Society of America. Proceedings* 41 (1986) 22. For the beginnings of such a theology see Mary Jo Leddy, "Exercising Theology in the Canadian Context," in Leddy and Hinsdale, eds., *Faith That Transforms: Essays in Honor of Gregory Baum* (New York: Paulist Press, 1987) 127-34; Christopher Lind, "An Invitation to Canadian Theology," *Toronto Journal of Theology* 1 (1985) 17-26.

[20]Leddy, "Exercising Theology in the Canadian Context," 129.

quent choice of conquest as a symbol of the relationship with the lost frontier in the literature of the United States.[21] Literary critics may disagree with Atwood's analysis of literature, but the symbol of survival does throw light on who we are as Canadians.

The survival of Canada as a nation is truly remarkable. Thirty years ago Northrop Frye wrote:

> In defiance of every geographical and economical law, Canada has made itself not simply a nation but an environment. It is only now emerging from its beginnings as a shambling, awkward, absurd country, groping and thrusting its way through incredible distances into the west and north, plundered by profiteers, interrupted by European wars, divided by language, and bedevilled by climate, yet slowly and inexorably bringing a culture to life.[22]

The struggle for survival as a nation described by Frye continues, and has been made explicit in the current debates on free trade. Even larger issues of survival face us, the survival of our planet and all its inhabitants, including humankind. Pollution, acid rain, irresponsible use of natural resources, militarism, and the possible future of annihilation through nuclear war or through some other form of environmental holocaust threaten the survival not only of individuals and nations, but of life itself as we know it.

A similar transition has taken place in feminist thought. Women have been identified with the body and with nature. The same attitudes of control and exploitation which have been directed towards women and the native peoples are also directed towards nature.[23] As feminists reject the hierarchical dualistic thinking which devalues the body and nature, they seek a more holistic understanding of humanness and of our relationship to nature. The experience of exploitation calls for a new approach to creation, an approach which recognizes our interconnectedness with all of creation and our co-responsibility for our world. As Sallie McFague rightly observes:

> The ecosystem of which we are part is a whole: the rocks and waters, atmosphere and soil, plants, animals, and human beings interact in dynamic, mutually supportive ways that make all talk of atomistic individualism indefensible. Relationship and interdependence, change and transformation, not substance, changelessness and perfection, are the categories within which a theology for our day must function.[24]

---

[21]Margaret Atwood, *Survival: A Thematic Guide to Canadian Literature* (Toronto: Anansi Press, 1972).

[22]Northrop Frye, ''Ned Pratt,'' in William Kilbourn, ed., *Canada: A Guide to the Peaceable Kingdom* (Toronto: MacMillan, 1970) 303.

[23]See Rosemary Radford Ruether, ''Ecology and Human Liberation: A Conflict between the Theology of History and the Theology of Nature?'' in *To Change the World: Christology and Cultural Criticism* (New York: Crossroad, 1981) 57-70.

[24]Sallie McFague, *Models of God: Theology for an Ecological, Nuclear Age* (Philadelphia: Fortress Press, 1987) 8. See also Rosemary Radford Ruether, ''Woman, Body, and Nature: Sexism and the Theology of Creation,'' in *Sexism and God-Talk: Toward a Feminist Theology* (Boston: Beacon Press, 1983) 72-92.

Rosemary Radford Ruether expresses the same conviction:

> We must start thinking of reality as the connecting links of a dance in which each part is equally vital to the whole, rather than the linear competition model in which the above prospers by defeating and suppressing what is below.[25]

The hierarchical patterns of relating to one another and to other forms of life need to be replaced by patterns of interdependence and mutuality. The transition from women's identification with nature to women's concern for ecology challenges how we view the world as well as the ways we theologize about God's relationship to that world and our responsibility for the future.[26]

Both the Canadian experience and the feminist experience are concerned with survival. For the first time in history humankind has the power to destroy ourselves and other forms of life. This terrifying situation demands a fresh theological response based on nurture and care rather than on domination.

Empowerment. The second transition taking place within our context is one of empowerment as Canadians move from being a colonial people to becoming an independent people with contributions to make to the global community. Canada has suffered and continues to suffer from a "colonial mentality," which takes it for granted that important decisions will be made elsewhere, in Paris, London, Washington, or New York, and for Catholics, in Rome. It is easy for us to fall into the "myth of our collective innocence," a "branch plant morality" which places moral and political responsibility elsewhere.[27] As Canadians we are challenged to grow up and to take responsibility not only for ourselves but as members of the world community with global responsibilities.

Canadians also need to acknowledge the colonies within our colony, particularly our native peoples who remain colonized. We are responsible for their continued colonization as well as for the ways that we contribute to the economic colonization of other peoples throughout the world. Our awareness of our interconnectedness must lead to actions which will empower those who still suffer the effects of colonization.

A parallel movement of empowerment is occurring as women move from a position of inferiority and domination to one of equality and full personhood.[28]

---

[25]Ruether, *To Change the World,* 67. Nature may be better understood in terms of plenitude and cooperation than in terms of scarcity and competition. See Michael Gross and Mary Beth Averill, "Evolution and Patriarchal Myths of Scarcity and Competition," in Harding and Hintikka, eds., *Discovering Reality,* 71-95.

[26]A dramatic instance of women's concern for ecology was described at the Third International Congress On Women which met in Dublin in 1987. Kamla Bhasin, Program Officer for the Food and Agricultural Organization in New Delhi, reported that women in northern India resisted deforestation by practicing *chipko* or "hugging the trees" which men were about to cut down, saying: "The trees are our sisters and brothers: if you wish to chop them down you must chop us first." See Paul Surlis, "Third International Congress on Women," *The Ecumenist* 26 (March-April 1988) 38.

[27]Leddy, "Exercising Theology in the Canadian Context," 133-34.

[28]Dorothee Sölle writes of the need for "liberation from colonialism" in her discussion of women's internalization of powerlessness, "Mysticism, Liberation and the Names of God," *Christianity and Crisis* 41 (1981) 181-82.

Such transformation begins with the refusal to be victim. In the words of the protagonist in Margaret Atwood's novel, *Surfacing*:

> This above all, to refuse to be a victim. Unless I can do that I can do nothing. I have to recant, give up the old belief that I am powerless and because of it nothing I can do will ever hurt anyone. . . . Withdrawal is no longer possible and the alternative is death.[29]

The process of empowerment involves dying to old ways of relating and awakening to a new consciousness of oneself as subject rather than as object. It demands a new understanding of power in relational terms and a recognition of our interrelatedness. This movement from powerlessness to empowerment calls for radical changes in family, church and society.

Liberation theologies, including feminist theologies, urge the whole church to make a "preferential option for the poor," the majority of whom are women: elderly women in single rooms afraid to go out, single mothers struggling to support their children, third world women unable to feed their families. Constance Parvey, in her essay on "Re-membering: A Global perspective on Women," asks:

> Is not the solidarity of the women's movement undermined by the very fact that it is educated and privileged women who have the *space* to speak, while silence is still the major "language" of those who are not admitted into the system, those who work for the lowest pay, the longest hours, in the least humanizing employment? Pornography and prostitution symbolize this silence, not making use of women's minds, but reducing women's bodies to objects governed by laws of supply and demand.[30]

The transition from powerlessness to empowerment must reach the poorest and the most abused women who are our sisters.

The Canadian experience of moving from colonial status to global responsibility and the movement for the liberation of women from a position of inferiority to one of full personhood can both be summed up by the word empowerment. This word symbolizes new approaches to power and new ways of relating to one another.

Pluralism. The Canadian experiment has been one of pluralism, based on compromise and continuity, characteristics necessary for survival. From our earliest days there has been an explicit commitment to protect minority rights. Unlike the United States, Canada has never made a dramatic break with the past. In 1867 confederation brought together four struggling colonies into a precarious union, balancing the claims of French and English, of Catholic and Protestant. It is significant that the British North America Act set up communal objectives of peace,

---

[29]Margaret Atwood, *Surfacing* (New York: Popular Library, 1972) 222-23.

[30]Constance F. Parvey, "Re-membering: A Global Perspective on Women," in Judith Weidman, ed., *Christian Feminism: Visions of a New Humanity* (San Francisco: Harper & Row, 1984) 165.

order and good government, in contrast to the more individualistic American objectives of life, liberty and the pursuit of happiness.[31]

The churches have been intimately involved in the political and social life of Canada from pioneer days to the present. Since there has been neither a "separation of church and state," nor any established religion, churches have been free to contribute to the life of the various communities both in grassroots activies as well as on the level of church leadership.[32] In the past twenty years much of this work has been done ecumenically. Many of the churches participate in inter-church coalitions. a particularly Canadian form of ecumenism which is believed to be unique in the world.[33]

Gregory Baum, commenting on "the alienation of many Americans in their institutions, their government, their political parties, their entire system," notes that: "In Canada, we are not as alienated from our institutions. We are not an empire, our institutions are more amenable to political actions."[34] It does seem that there is in Canada a more tolerant attitude toward religious and moral diversity.[35] The experience of pluralism and of working together for a solution has been part of Canadian history from its beginning with our two founding nations and has continued with the subsequent arrival of persons from many cultures.

Just as Canada has grown from the recognition of two cultures to an acceptance of cultural pluralism, a similar transition has taken place within the history

---

[31]For an analysis of differences between Canada and United States from a political science perspective see O. Kruhlak, R. Schultz, and S. Pobihushchy, eds., *The Canadian Political Process* (Toronto: Holt, Rinehart and Winston of Canada, 1970), especially S. M. Lipset, "Revolution and Counterrevolution: The United States and Canada," 13-38, and G. Horowitz, "Conservatism, Liberalism, and Socialism in Canada: An Interpretation," 47-74.

[32]Canadian Catholics have had good leadership in the Canadian Conference of Catholic Bishops since its inception in 1943. Because there is no "separation of church and state" the Catholic bishops have been recognized as a legitimate institution in the political and social fabric of the nation, representing 47 per cent of the Canadian population (25 per cent francophone, 22 percent anglophone). The two sectors of the Conference, the francophone and the anglophone, have had to develop the skills of working together while respecting legitimate differences. See E. Sheridan, ed., *Do Justice! The Social Teaching of the Canadian Catholic Bishops (1945-1986)* (Toronto: Jesuit Centre for Social Faith and Justice, 1987); Gregory Baum, *Compassion and Solidarity: The Church for Others* (Toronto: CBC Enterprises, 1987).

[33]Remi De Roo, Bishop of Victoria, describes these coalitions in *Cries of Victims—Voice of God* (Ottawa: Novalis, 1986) 95-105.

[34]Gregory Baum, "The Grand Vision: It Needs Social Action," in Anne Lonergan and Caroline Richards, eds., *Thomas Berry and the New Cosmology* (Mystic CT: Twenty-Third Publications, 1987) 54- 55.

[35]This tolerance, as well as less interest in evangelism, is noted by George Gallup in his foreword to Reginald Bibby, *Fragmented Gods: The Poverty and Potential of Religion in Canada* (Toronto: Irwin Publishing, 1987) ix. Reginald Bibby considers that history has produced two very different religious marketplaces in North America: Canada, characterized by an effort to achieve working agreements among diverse parties, and the United States with its aggressive, persistent claims to truth (215-18).

of the women's movement which may be seen as a transition from woman's special role or moral mission to the recognition of different voices. Our nineteenth century foremothers were convinced that they had special gifts which were needed in the public domain. They resolutely worked for the inclusion of women in public life. Feminists today reject the complementary view of female and male which speaks of "woman's special nature" and which assigns to women a "special role," but they insist on the recognition of the diversity of women's experience. As Anne Carr emphasizes: "Since the experience of women is particular and varied, feminist theology is radically pluralist. Each voice is only one in a wider conversation."[36] Women of color and third world women have raised their voices. Women are striving to learn to hear the different voices in the conversation and to accept alternative traditions.[37]

The ability to work within existing structures with persons who have very different perspectives may be seen in Canadian feminism.[38] The institutions of state and church are viewed as potentially emancipatory. For example, the Royal Commission on the Status of Women set up by the Canadian government in 1967 helped to mobilize women's groups and to shift public attitudes towards women's issues. The dialogue of women with the Canadian Conference of Catholic Bishops has had somewhat the same results within the Canadian Catholic Church.[39] Both in the larger society and in the church there is a willingness for different groups of women who do not share the same vision to work together on a common project and to share their different visions.[40]

There are deep divisions both within Canadian society and within the women's movement, and yet the experience of working with groups that have different languages, different histories, different traditions in ways that contribute to the good of all has marked our history. The word that describes this experience is pluralism. The lesson is desperately needed in our global village. "If we do not learn to live together we will die together."[41]

---

[36]Anne E. Carr, *Transforming Grace: Christian Tradition and Women's Experience* (San Francisco: Harper & Row, 1988) 166.

[37]For some examples of this conversation with women from different contexts see Letty Russell, ed., *Inheriting Our Mother's Gardens: Feminist Theology in Third World Perspective* (forthcoming); The Amencida Collective, Carter Heyward, Anne Gilson, eds., *Revolutionary Forgiveness: Feminist Reflections on Nicaragua* Maryknoll, NY: Orbis, 1987); Janet Silman, ed., *Enough is Enough: Aboriginal Women Speak Out* (Toronto: The Women's Press, 1987).

[38]For information on feminism in Canada see Roberta Hamilton and Michele Barrett, eds., *The Politics of Diversity: Feminism, Marxism and Nationalism* (Montreal: Book Centre, 1986), especially the Introduction.

[39]See Elisabeth Lacelle, "From Today to Tomorrow: Women in the Canadian Catholic Church," in *Grail: An Ecumenical Journal* 1 (1985) 25-32 and the recommendations of the Canadian Conference of Catholic Bishops on "Role of Women in the Church," 33-35.

[40]Hamilton and Barrett note this: " . . . Canadians talk to each other—indeed shout at each other—across barriers of theory, analysis and politics that in Britain, for example, would long since have created an angry truce of silent pluralism." *The Politics of Diversity*, 1.

[41]McFague, *Models of God*, 53.

III. THESE EXPERIENCES AS SOURCE FOR THEOLOGY

In Part II, I have described three transitional experiences which may be summarized as survival, empowerment. and pluralism. I turn now to how these Canadian and feminist experiences have caused me to rethink my theology, particularly my image of God and my understanding of anthropology, christology, and ecclesiology. This is a formidable task which is very much in process. In the time that remains I will suggest some directions for revisioning in each of these areas.

Image of God. In the face of nuclear destruction, are our ways of thinking and talking about God, and God's relationship to the world, helpful or harmful for our survival? Do they contribute to domination or to empowerment? Do they reflect the rich diversity of human experience, especially the experience of those who have been excluded? These questions lead to a critique of the imagery used for God in theology and in liturgy.

The image of a white male God over against the world has legitimated many forms of oppression. This was illustrated by Mary Daly twenty years ago in her powerful critique, *Beyond God the Father*.[42] The feminist critique of language about God and reformulations in the light of women's experience leads to a new awareness of the absolute mystery who embraces all creation. The process is described in a vivid way by Alice Walker in *The Color Purple* as Celie, a black woman who has suffered great oppression, gradually comes to a new vision of God and herself.

> Trying to chase that old white man out of my head. I been so busy thinking bout him I never truly notice nothing God made. Not a blade of corn (how it do that?) not the color purple (where it come from?). Not the wildflowers. Nothing.

But as Celie experienced, " . . . this hard work, let me tell you. He been there so long, he don't want to budge. He threaten lightening, floods and earthquakes."[43]

The issue of survival makes this "hard work" crucial. The almost exclusively male imagery which envisions God as father, king, lord, and master suggests a one-sidedly masculine transcendent God who is "in charge." Such images easily lead to either militarism (God is on our side) or escapism (God will take care of us). Neither view encourages human responsibility for the world. A God who suffers with the world and who shares responsibility with us for its survival provides a corrective to the image of a powerful transcendent God distant from creation.

The new consciousness of women as image of God has encouraged the use of female imagery for God. This imagery frees the idea of divine transcendence from its notion of domination and provides a more holistic view of God's relationship with the world, a view which empowers women and men to assume their responsibility for this world. We need to critique not only the nouns that we use for God. but also the verbs with which we describe God's activity. Words such as direct,

---

[42]See Mary Daly, *Beyond God the Father: Toward a Philosophy of Women's Liberation* (Boston: Beacon Press, 1973).

[43]Alice Walker, *The Color Purple* (New York: Washington Square Press, 1982) 179.

control, rule, judge, destroy, overcome, describe a God who dominates while verbs such as empower, liberate, nourish, support, enliven, leave room for our human response to a God who invites us to be responsible.[44] Even the structure of the language that we use for God needs to be rethought in the light of Mary Daly's presentation of God as Verb. The urgency of our present situation calls for images of God which encourage us, who are made in God's image, to assume responsibility for our world which is God's world and to discover ways of relating to one another which are empowering.[45]

The rich diversity of human experience invites the use of multiple images for God. As Elizabeth Johnson suggests: "The very incomprehensibility of God demands a proliferation of images and a variety of names, each of which acts as a corrective against the tendency of any one to become reified and literal."[46] The use of many different images for God purifies our God-talk of literalism and even idolatry.

Recognizing that all language about God is metaphorical, Sallie McFague proposes that the world be imaged as God's body. In place of triumphalist, monarchical, patriarchal models for God, she develops the models of God as mother, lover, and friend of the world.[47] These images of God are found in our tradition, although they are less prominent than those which refer to God as father, lord, and king.[48] It is the task of theology to revision God in the light of contemporary experience, especially the experience of the excluded ones. The message of Jesus seems to have been that such persons are a privileged presence of God in our midst.

Anthropology and Christology. The issue of survival, the transformation from domination to empowerment, and the acceptance of pluralism, not only challenge our images of God but also how we understand ourselves, made in God's image. We look to anthropology and christology and realize that these have been based on "only partial human experience only partially understood." As those who have been excluded reflect on their experience and on the Christian tradition they become aware that the tradition has legitimated domination by certain groups who have imposed servitude on other groups.[49] Such attitudes of domination threaten

---

[44]Dorothee Sölle discusses the relationship between language and liberation in "Mysticism, Liberation and the Names of God," 179-85.

[45]John B. Cobb in a joint work with David Tracy, *Talking About God: Doing Theology in the Context of Modern Pluralism* (New York: Seabury Press, 1983) explores how the challenges of modernity, including the challenge of feminism, provide resources for this task.

[46]Elizabeth A. Johnson, "The Incomprehensibility of God and the Image of God Male and Female," *Theological Studies* 45 (1984) 444.

[47]McFague, *Models of God.*

[48]See Phyllis Trible, *God and the Rhetoric of Sexuality* (Philadelphia: Fortress Press, 1978); Mary Rose D'Angelo, "Beyond Father and Son," in C. Lind and T. Brown, eds., *Justice as Mission: An Agenda for the Church* (Burlington, Ontario: Trinity Press, 1985) 108-19; Sandra M. Schneiders, *Women and the Word: The Gender of God in the New Testament and the Spirituality of Women* (New York: Paulist Press, 1986).

[49]For a study of how this took place in early Christianity see Elisabeth Schüssler Fiorenza, *In Memory of Her: A Feminist Theological Reconstruction of Christian Origins* (New York: Crossroad, 1983).

our survival. We need to discover ways of relating to one another that are mutually empowering and that are open to the many voices in our world.

An example of how experience suggests the need for reinterpretation of symbols and doctrines may be seen in feminist understandings of sin and salvation. The experience of sin is different for those who are powerless than it is for those with power. The traditional emphasis on sin as pride and rebellion against God does not fit the experience of those whose self has been devalued by the dominant culture and who consequently lack a sense of self. Sin for such persons is the passive acceptance of their situation while salvation involves transformation from being victims to becoming responsible subjects. Feminist theology suggests that both sin and salvation need to be rethought in ways that are relational, communitarian, and pluralistic.[50]

This understanding of sin and salvation is based on an awareness of our solidarity with all humankind, and with all of creation. Such solidarity, as Metz insists, is not only with the present but with the past and future, a "backward solidarity" with the silent and forgotten dead, as well as a "forward solidarity" with coming generations.[51] Salvation needs to embrace all of creation in a way that empowers all of us to build our future.

For Christians Jesus is the Christ, the one who empowers us to do this. However, feminist scholarship shows that the Christian story has been handed down (recorded, interpreted, analyzed) in ways that are oppressive for women. At the same time the Bible and tradition have been and are a source of wisdom and liberation for women. The present experience of women, who find within their religious tradition sources both of oppression and of liberation, becomes the hermeneutical principle for judging what is empowering. The Bible, and Jesus himself, are viewed as historical prototype rather than mythical archetype.[52] In this way they are a resource for the present as Christian women remember the domination of our sisters, but also celebrate their wisdom and courage.

The figure of Jesus, often seen as the legitimator of male superiority, is revealed in the gospels as one who renounced domination and who sought to empower those on the margins of society. Christ as body includes all the baptized, black and white, young and old, female and male. Rosemary Radford Ruether poses this question:

---

[50]Anne Carr, *Transforming Grace,* 186-87. For an example of such theologizing from third world women's perspective see the final document of the intercontinental conference of women theologians from the third world which met in Oaxtepec, Mexico, December 1986. They wrote: "Suffering that is inflicted by the oppressor and is passively accepted does not lead to life; it is destructive and demonic. But suffering which is part of the struggle for the sake of God's Reign or which results from the uncontrollable and mysterious conditions of humankind, is redeeming and is rooted in the Paschal Mystery, evocative of the rhythm of pregnancy, delivery, and birth." *Fish-Eye Lens* (April 1988) 20.

[51]Metz, *Faith in History and Society,* 130.

[52]Elisabeth Schüssler Fiorenza, "Emerging Issues in Feminist Biblical Interpretation," in *Christian Feminism,* 33-54; see also Rosemary Radford Ruether, *Sexism and God-Talk,* 134-38.

As our perception of our incompleteness changes with new sensitivities to racism, sexism, and European chauvinism, must not the image of Christ take ever new forms: as woman, as Black and Brown woman, as impoverished and despised woman of those peoples who are the underside of Christian imperialism?[53]

The answer is surely yes, we must discover Christ in our sisters as well as our brothers. Rather than being a symbol of domination, the Christ or the Christa can be a symbol of empowerment.[54]

But theology must also consider the effects that Christian symbols and doctrines have had in history. As Anne Carr indicates,

Feminist reflection on the doctrines of God and of Christ that shows that God is not male and that Jesus' maleness is a purely contingent fact must further attend to the effective history of these doctrines, their practical and political uses. Only if the effects of these symbols and doctrines are transformed now and in the future can it be claimed that the symbols and doctrines are not intrinsically patriarchal, and that they can be made available to women.[55]

Carr here issues a challenge to systematic theology and to practice in the church. Unless it can be met, we cannot speak of Christianity as a redemptive possibility.

Ecclesiology. The place where mutual empowerment should take place is the church. However, relationships within the church, both on a local and a universal level, often reflect the divisions in society, rather than the empowering Spirit of Jesus. This is true of the relationships of women and men within the church. For this reason the World Council of Churches has launched a world-wide ecumenical decade from 1988 to 1998 on the theme of "Churches in Solidarity with Women" in order to consider how churches can empower women to claim their full humanity. The concern is two-fold: the position of women in the churches and the churches' responsibility to improve the conditions of women in society as a whole. This concern is not a "women's issue" but an ecclesiological issue which bears on the nature and mission of the church.

An ecclesiology which begins with contemporary experience must draw on the experience of local Christian communities.[56] Catholic ecclesiology of the past and even the ecclesiology of Vatican II is challenged by the different experiences of

---

[53]*Womanguides: Readings Toward a Feminist Theology* (Boston: Beacon Press, 1985) 112-13.

[54]For "Reflections on the Christa," see *Journal of Women and Religion* 4 (1985), particularly Edwina Hunter, 22-32.

[55]Carr, *Transforming Grace,* 109.

[56]As Joseph Komonchak states, the church is "always first of all a concrete reality, *this* group of men and women, at *this* time and in *this* place, within *this* culture, responding to the Word and grace by which God gathers them in Christ." "The Church Universal as the Communion of Local Churches," in G. Alberigo and G. Gutiérrez, eds., *Where Does the Church Stand? Concilium* 146 (New York: Seabury Press, 1981) 32. For a more developed presentation on the emergence of the local church and the eucharistic community as starting point for ecclesiology see my forthcoming articles on "Differing Gifts" and "Differing Responses to Mission," "Theological Trends in Ecclesiology," *The Way* 28 (1988).

church coming from Africa, Asia, Latin America, and women gathered as church.[57] The question raised by Metz, "Can the 'church for the people' become the 'church of the people'?" still needs to be answered.[58] As he insists, it is not just that people need theology—but theology needs the self-expression of people—their symbols, stories, and collective memories.[59] It especially needs to hear from those who have been silent. Their voices may show us how the Spirit is forming the church in our day.

There are numerous examples of previously "muted ones" gathering as church. I will mention only two. In September 1987, 10,000 *campesinos* from remote mountain villages in Peru met for two days of reflection and prayer in a Theological Eucharistic Congress in which they spoke their theology and proclaimed: "We are the people. We are the church."[60] In a very different context 3000 women and some men from twenty-five countries and a variety of denominations met in Cincinnati, Ohio, in October 1987 as "Women-Church Claiming Our Power." But even more significant than these large ecclesial gatherings are the small ecclesial communities in many parts of the world where Christians are articulating their theology and discovering what it means for them to be church.[61] These experiences of empowerment and of diversity express the richness of unity in faith.[62]

However, the church does not exist for itself, but for the world. Christians from different traditions are coming together as church in response to the needs of the world. The issue of survival urges Christian churches to enter into the wider ecumenism with other religions. The task of working together in ways that respect differences challenges the church today if it is to be truly a "world church" which contributes to the unity of humankind.

To sum up, ecclesiologies for our age must take seriously the threats to our survival as they reflect on the church's mission to the world. The church should facilitate the empowerment of all persons if it is to be true to its nature as "uni-

---

[57]As Tissa Balasuriya observes: "Christianity is only now beginning the process of purifying itself from being the religion of the Holy Roman Empire, Western culture, and Euro-American capitalism." *Planetary Theology,* 121. For reflection on women gathering as church see Rosemary Radford Ruether, *Women-Church: Theology and Practice of Feminist Liturgical Communities* (San Francisco: Harper & Row, 1985).

[58]Metz, "Church and People: The Forgotten Subject of Faith," in *Faith in History and Society,* 136-53.

[59]Ibid., 148.

[60]Greg Chisholm describes this gathering in "Sow Life to Reap Peace," *Scarboro Missions* 69 (1988) 20-22.

[61]For theological reflection on the experience of base communities, see Rahner, "Basic Communities," *Theological Investigations* 19 (New York: Crossroads, 1983) 159-65; Alvaro Barreiro, *Basic Ecclesial Communities: The Evangelization of the Poor* (Maryknoll, NY: Orbis, 1984); Leonardo Boff, *Church: Charism and Power* (New York: Crossroad, 1985); Boff, *Ecclesiogenesis* (New York: Orbis, 1987); Marcello de Azevedo, "Basic Communities: A Meeting Point of Ecclesiologies," *Theological Studies* 46 (1985) 601-20.

[62]See Yves Congar, *Diversity and Communion* (Mystic, CT: Twenty-Third Publications, 1985) for a study of diversity of customs and opinions which have been accepted in the unity of faith.

versal sacrament of salvation.'' And finally, ecclesiologies must reflect the pluralism of our experiences of church. In place of the pyramid, Letty Russell suggests the image of the rainbow as a paradigm for diversity and inclusivity within the church.[63] It is a fitting image, since it is also a symbol of God's promise to humankind.

CONCLUSION

In Part III, I have suggested some of the ways that attention to particular experiences can help us to revision our images of God, humanity, Christ, and church. In conclusion I wish to stress that by listening to the stories of various groups, we discover how God is revealing God's self today. The theologians' task is to listen with attention and humility to what God is doing in our complex world. New voices are being raised and these voices need to be heard. This is an important step in the process of discernment. It is not enough that the new voices speak to one another. As David Tracy writes:

> . . . the voices of the others multiply—all those considered ''non-persons'' by the powerful but declared by the great prophets to be God's own privileged ones. All the victims of our discourses and our history have begun to discover their own discourses in ways that our discourse finds difficult to hear, much less listen to. Their voices can seem strident and uncivil—in a word other. And they are. We have all just begun to sense the terror of that otherness. But only by beginning to listen to those other voices may we also begin to hear the otherness within our own discourse and within ourselves. What we then might begin to hear, above our chatter, are possibilities we have never dared to dream.[64]

Such a willingness to listen actively and critically demands conversion.

I find myself listening and speaking both as privileged and as outsider, privileged as a North American, and yet sharing some of the experiences of the outsider. Canadians have historically been the victims of other empires and women have historically been ''voiceless'' in the discourses of faith and politics. These ''muted voices'' need to be heard in interpreting our faith and in shaping our future. The correction of bias in the use of experience as a source for theology includes an option for the oppressed who are God's privileged ones.

As I listen to my own experience as a Canadian and as a woman, I have discovered that the Canadian experience of survival, overcoming of a colonial mentality, and acceptance of pluralism, paralleled by a feminist concern for ecology, empowerment, and respect for different voices contributes to a theology which uses present experience as a source, particularly the experiences of those who have been ignored or devalued. I discover that it is possible to understand the larger issues through the personal and the particular. In my experience as a Canadian woman I recognize God's presence calling me to be responsible for this world, to work for the empowerment of all peoples, and especially of women, and to listen

---

[63]Letty Russell, ''Women and Ministry: Problem or Possibility,'' in *Christian Feminism*, 75-92.

[64]David Tracy, *Plurality and Ambiguity: Hermeneutics, Religion, Hope* (San Francisco: Harper & Row, 1987) 79.

to the voices of my sisters and brothers in my local community and in the larger world community.[65]

ELLEN LEONARD, C.S.J.
University of St. Michael's College, Toronto

---

[65]After this address a participant who had worked in L'Arche communities spoke to me of his concern that we learn to listen to the voices of those who are physically unable to speak. Such people are an extreme example of muted voices.

A RESPONSE TO ELLEN LEONARD

Experience is such an elusive yet evocative term. Presumably, the term refers mainly to the actual living through of an event, the actual enjoyment of suffering and, hence, the effect upon our human judgment and feelings produced by direct and personal knowledge through impressions. We speak of a special knowledge *by experience* of pain, delusion, joy, love as opposed to inference or hearsay or mere external authority. We also use the term, experience, to refer to practical knowledge and practical reason, the skilled knowing of embodied, "tacit," knowledge. The resonance of experience turns Newman's *notional* into *real* assent. Yes, of course, we know there is no unmediated, unthematized or unsymbolized experience but experience adds something to the themes, symbols and languages which are its necessary medium.

In some sense, all of theology, as wisdom, is reflection on experience. Indeed, experience is the foundational test of revelation and tradition because the latter claims to bear a universal message to humanity, to represent the normatively human. Hence, theologians speak of a necessary method of mutual critical correlation between experience and revelation. And when revelation and the tradition do not jibe, something is a-kilter.

Perhaps if we did not divide spirituality and theology in the artificial ways we often do, we would have long since mined the personal experience of our own prayer and discerned feelings and faith narratives and that, too, of the saints and mystics as theological test and source. Recently, one of our members, William Thompson has carefully and brilliantly appealed to this religion of experience in his new book, *Fire and Light: The Saints and Theology,* to show how experience in prayer does more than merely confirm or illuminate by giving depth to what we already really know.[1]

Ellen Leonard asserts in her very good paper that "the recovery of *present* experience in its full social and political dimensions" is foundational for theology. Leonard's emphasis on experience as primarily communal (for what would private experience or a private language really mean?) is very salutary against pervasive tendencies in the United States (I do not speak of Canada) to equate experience with the individual, the personal, the psychological. We have William James' classic, *The Varieties of Religious Experience,* to blame for this individualistic aberration.[2] James also too much—following the pattern set in the United

---

[1]William Thompson, *Fire and Light: The Saints and Theology* (New York: Paulist Press, 1987).

[2]William James, *The Variety of Religious Experiences* (New York: Longmans, Green, 1923).

States by the evangelical revivalistic tradition—stresses experience as extraordinary, as "peak" experience, as opposed to the much more mundane, ordinary experience in which God is mainly found. In a healthy reaction, Ellen Leonard stresses the contextual—for all experience is contextual so that we need to ask, "whose experience" and experience from what place and social location?—so Leonard illustrates her point by drawing on women's experience and Canadian contextual experience.

Experience is communal. Even as individuals we mainly live off of the great collective symbols to make sense of life. Moreover, most experiences are contrast experiences! Without contrast, our experience remains unreflected, unnoticed like the air we breathe, the experience of the primitive people which the anthropologist Edward Stanner calls "in the dreaming." Conflict—or, at least, contact— with the other—precisely as other—is the pre-condition for any experience at all. Leonard speaks of the contrast between the dominant and the muted groups in speaking of women. The latter are a species of "deviant insiders"—like Jews, classically, or other pariah people (as Max Weber noted) or gays, women, too, see the world of patriarchical domination with double eyes, with a two-fold language, with divided loyalties, belonging to two communities, two narratives. Perhaps one reason for the modern infatuation with experience is that we *all* (in the global village) now belong to multiple traditions, loyalties, communities, narratives. We all feel like deviant insiders within our churches, universities, communities. For all of us, modernity—with its pluralism of traditions made available—means that, like Ghandi, we have to "experiment with truth." Hence, the upgraded saliency of experience in theology.

Leonard stresses the contrast experience of marginalized and dominant communities. But another, perhaps, even more ordinary source of contrast experience comes from what Alfred Schutz, the sociologist refers to as the world of everyday life (the life-world of direct, pragmatic coping in the world through the maxims of common wisdom) and the more specialized domains of science and other "second" (second because reflective) languages such as theology, aesthetics, the social sciences.[3] Second languages raise the issue of experience since all second languages, such as theology, are always derivative, a bit conjectural, need testing in and by experience.

Usually, as Thomas Kuhn reminds us in *The Structure of Scientific Revolutions*) changes in a scientific paradigm (in any second language) comes less from individual experiences (as in and through controlled experiments) than from communal changes in the life-world of scientific communication.[4] On his part, Michel Foucault thinks that contrast experiences (as personal experiences) do little more than uncover and recognize the decay of epochal cultural thematics and hasten their demise.[5] So, contrast experiences, too, are largely contextual, communal, generational.

---

[3]Alfred Schutz, "Of Multiple Realities," *Collected Papers* I (The Hague: Martinus Nijhoff, 1962).

[4]Thomas Kuhn, *The Structure of Scientific Revolutions* (2nd. ed.; Chicago: University of Chicago Press, 1970).

[5]Michel Foucault, *Power/Knowledge* (New York: Pantheon Books, 1981).

It will be in Leonard's emphases on experience as communal and contrast experience that we will find clues to help us sort out authentic from inauthentic, humanizing from de-humanizing experiences. I would have liked a bit more attention to this issue in Leonard's paper. Experience, to be sure, tests the received traditions. If they do not ring true to the received traditions, either the experience is flawed or parts of the tradition have been forgotten and need retrieving or been truncated and need expanding. Experience as a category and expectation challenges all closed systems and too universal claims, even for revelation!

Ellen Leonard asks, rightly, whose experiences shall count and answers, pluralistically, everyone's, in a non-coerced communication and listening. Well and good. But what of the delusions in our experience or the narrow range to it? How are we to engage in that active and critical listening to our own experiences and that of others which Leonard calls us to? We have various therapies (psychological and spiritual) to help us discern personal experiences and correct, overcome and/or affirm them. We need something like Jonathan Edwards' treatise on the nature of true religious affections—i.e., a discernment model—to bring to the issue of experience.

So, too, we will need various criteria to help us know what from local context is to be affirmed, what opposed. Without expounding on them, I think the moves we find in Robert Schreiter's little gem of a book, *Constructing Local Theologies*—especially his section on "criteria for Christian identity"—might help us discern where context is enrichment, even deeper revelation, of the gospel and where deformation.[6] For after we have discussed Ellen Leonard's distributive justice criterion, "whose experience counts in theological reflection," we will need to press a bit more than she does toward more substantive questions: not just whose but what sort of experience will count as authentically Christian experience?

But, to avoid any too quick foreclosure on this question, we will need to heed the kind of humility Leonard calls for in the end of her paper. The experience of the other—the boat refuge, the holocaust survivor, the recovering alcoholic, the AIDS patient, the welfare mother—humbles and corrects my own limited and biased experience. But also the experiences of past generations relativizes our *present* experience (although, of course, it can only come alive again by becoming embodied in our experience). And, finally, the mysterious God who can not be, as mystery, defined or encapsulated—yet, perhaps, she can be experienced—puts in question marks any easy closure of human experience. That, it seems to me, is what those who sleight human experience as a locus for theology implicitly do. As always, the denial or minimization of any authentic human experience is an implicit denial of the mystery of God. And for this very reason—as Leonard reminds us—looking to experience as a source for theology is no luxury for those traditionalists, like myself, who insist that theology is, ultimately, about the experience (as limit and disclosure) of the mysterious God.

JOHN A. COLEMAN
The Jesuit School of Berkeley

[6]Robert Schreiter, *Constructing Local Theologies* Maryknoll, NY: Orbis, 1985) 117-23).

MAGISTERIUM AND THEOLOGY

At some point in my preparation of this paper it occurred to me that the theme chosen for this convention was substantially the one that Melchior Cano had treated over four centuries ago in his famous work *De Locis Theologicis*.[1] I have to confess I had never had this book in my hands before, but I was moved to take a look to see how he had treated the question, and I found it rather worthwhile to do so. The first thing I noted was that he did not speak of Scripture and apostolic tradition as two *fontes,* but as the two *loci* where all revealed truths, all the *principia propria* for theology, are to be found. After these he named five *loci* which interpret what is contained in Scripture and Tradition. Of these five, the first three, which offer certain arguments for theology, are the faith-consensus of the Catholic Church, doctrinal decisions of general councils, and doctrinal decisions of the popes; the other two, offering probable arguments, are the writings of the fathers and of theologians.[2]

In Melchior Cano's terminology, then, I will be speaking of the magisterium as a *locus theologicus*. To put it more specifically, I'll be speaking of the second and third of his *loci interpretativi:* namely, the magisterium as exercised by councils and by popes. And I'll be asking much the same questions that Cano was asking: what is the significance of these *loci* for theology? How should theologians make use of them?

Speaking of using them raises the question of where one finds them. Well, for the councils we have the various collections of *Acta,* and for the popes we have the *Bullarium* and the *Acta Apostolicae Sedis.* But for common every-day consultation, I'm sure most of us would turn to our copy of Denzinger. So I'm going to make my question very concrete by phrasing it this way: what is the significance of Denzinger's *Enchiridion* as a collection of *loci* for Catholic theology today?

If we rightly share Karl Rahner's disdain for what he called "Denzinger-theology,"[3] does that mean that what is contained between the covers of Denzinger's *Enchiridion* has no more importance for our work as Catholic theologians? Karl Rahner, for one, did not think so. Indeed he thought Denzinger important enough to devote a good deal of his own time during his productive years between 1952

---

[1]Melchior Cano died in 1560; his *De Locis Theologicis* was first published at Salamanca in 1563.

[2]See especially Lib. I, Cap. 3 and Lib. XII, Cap. 2.

[3]Karl Rahner, "Membership of the Church according to the Teaching of Pius XII's Encyclical 'Mystici Corporis Christi,' " *Theological Investigations* 2 (London: Darton Longman and Todd, 1963) 2, n.2.

and 1957, to seeing the 28th, 29th, 30th and 31st editions through the press. He wanted this hand-book to be kept up-to-date and to be improved, not, obviously, for the perpetuation of what he called "Denzinger-theology," but out of his profound respect for its contents, and his Catholic sense of the proper weight to be given to the documents of the magisterium. It also was Rahner who arranged to have Adolf Schönmetzer take over the task of preparing new editions when he could no longer do it himself. I feel sure that you have profited from the very considerable improvements that Fr. Schönmetzer made in subsequent editions, especially in the historical and critical introductions he provided for so many of the texts. Perhaps not many are aware of the fact that the kind of painstaking work he did in preparing the 32nd to the 36th edition of Denzinger eventually cost him his eyesight. I'm sure he would have been the last person in the world to want people to use the fruit of his labor just to do "Denzinger-theology," which Rahner described as a theology that limits itself to defending and commenting on the clear and explicit doctrinal pronouncements of the magisterium.[4] As Yves Congar has pointed out, the way to avoid the stigma of doing "Denzinger-theology" is not by throwing this book out, but by using it correctly.[5]

But before going into the question of its proper usage, let us recall what it contains. The full title reads: *Enchiridion Symbolorum, Definitionum Declarationum*. So we have here three different kinds of documents: baptismal creeds, solemn definitions, and a variety of non-definitive statements of the magisterium. Since each of these is really a different kind of *locus* for theology, it will be helpful to consider each separately.

BAPTISMAL CREEDS

The first one hundred numbers in the recent editions of Denzinger are reserved for the professions of faith that were used in the liturgy, especially of baptism, during the early centuries. They constitute a priceless witness to the way the apostolic faith was handed on from generation to generation in the churches: a witness all the more impressive in that they show that at the time when there was no one uniform creed being used everywhere, the creeds of the particular churches manifest a common faith. We don't know who composed these ancient creeds, but they can rightly be described as documents of the magisterium, since it was the bishops, presiding over the liturgy of baptism, who were responsible for the faith which the candidates for baptism were called upon to profess.

The early baptismal creeds constitute a primary *locus* for theology, since they are such authentic witnesses to the faith of which theology seeks understanding. In a broad sense one can say that the major purpose of all subsequent interventions of the magisterium has been to explicitate, clarify and defend the true sense in which various articles of the baptismal creed are to be understood. One can also say that what we theologians are seeking is a deeper understanding of the faith in which we ourselves were baptized.

---

[4]Rahner, "Membership of the Church," 2.

[5]Yves Congar, "Du bon usage de 'Denzinger,' " in *Situations et taches presentes de la théologie* (Paris: Cerf, 1967) 111-33.

Reflection on these baptismal creeds reminds us that it is through the church in which we were baptized that we have received the faith we are seeking to understand. Our faith has to be ecclesial faith, or it will not be Christian faith at all. It follows that our theology, as reflection on our own faith, is necessarily ecclesial as well. As we ourselves are believers only as committed members of a community of faith, so also we work as Catholic theologians as committed participants in the faith, life and worship of the Catholic Church. As Avery Dulles has pointed out: "To be a true theologian, one must dwell in spirit within the community of faith; one must participate in the Christian symbols and in their meaning for the community. This kind of participatory knowledge will make it possible to see the formulas in relation to the unexplicit meaning which they carry for those who share in the tradition."[6]

The *credo ecclesiam* of our baptismal profession means that we look upon the church with the eyes of faith. We see the church as the fruit of Christ's definitive victory over the powers of evil, assured of the abiding presence of the Holy Spirit, the Spirit of truth that will lead her into all the truth. Our *credo ecclesiam* means also that we believe that the episcopal and papal structure of the Catholic Church corresponds to God's design for his church. We believe that the authority with which bishops and popes lead and teach in the church comes to them ultimately from Christ, and that in the exercise of their office they enjoy a special assistance of the Holy Spirit, in virtue of which we believe that when they teach in a definitive way they will not lead the church into serious errors in its faith, and that even in their non-definitive teaching they provide generally reliable witness to the faith of the church.

A practical consequence of all this is that we approach the *Documenta magisterii ecclesiastici* which constitute the rest of Benzinger's *Enchiridion*, with an attitude of faith. We come prepared to offer our *obsequium fidei* to what we find there as defined dogma; and to offer the appropriate degree of *obsequium religiosum* to what is taught there authoritatively but not definitively.

We also approach these documents as theologians, and that means our approach must also be methodical, systematic, critical. One of the first questions we will want to ask is: of all the eight hundred or so documents collected here, which ones contain "definitions" and which are merely "declarations" (the generic term used in the title for all non-definitive statements of the magisterium)? In his introduction, Schönmetzer mentions the fact that some people had suggested to him that he use some editorial device to mark out the dogmatic definitions from everything else in the enchiridion.[7] Needless to say he wisely refused to take up this challenge. But it is a challenge that Catholic theology cannot ignore.

Indeed it is a primary task of theology to establish the criteria by which defined dogmas can be distinguished from all other statements of doctrine, and then, by applying these criteria, to identify the definitions that call for our *obsequium fidei*.

---

[6]Avery Dulles, "The church, Sacrament and Ground of Faith," in Rene Latourelle and Gerald O'Collins, eds., *Problems and Perspectives of Fundamental Theology* (New York/Ramsey: Paulist, 1982) 272.

[7]34th edition (Barcelona: Herder, 1967) 7.

Since solemn definitions constitute a special *locus theologicus,* demanding a response and critical reflection that will be quite different from what is appropriate as regards statements of the ordinary magisterium, let us consider these two kinds of statements separately.

DOGMATIC DEFINITIONS AS A LOCUS FOR THEOLOGY

An outstanding example of the kind of work that needs to be done to establish the criteria by which dogmatic definitions can be identified, has been provided by the research that Piet Fransen and others have done on the meaning of such terms as *fides, haeresis, anathema sit,* in the documents of the Council of Trent.[8] This research has shown conclusively that Trent defined far fewer dogmas, in the modern sense of this term, than was previously thought to be the case. No doubt much further work along this line needs to be done. Here, then, is a critical task for theology, and one in which church historians will play an indispensable role as well.

What kind of statements will theology identify as dogmatic definitions? One essential quality of such statements is that they are professions of faith. When councils define dogmas of faith they do not say: "We decree such and such," but rather: "We believe such and such." When they use the term: "We define," they are giving to the faithful a solemn assurance that something has been revealed by God; the assent that is called for is not to the definers, but to the truth as revealed, and hence to God who has revealed it.

When the magisterium defines a doctrine as divinely revealed, it implicitly defines that this doctrine is objectively contained in what *Dei Verbum* calls "the sacred deposit of the Word of God," which is committed to the church in the form of Scripture and Tradition (DV 10). To quote a memorable passage of the same Constitution: "This teaching office is not above the word of God, but serves it, teaching only what has been handed on, listening to it devoutly, guarding it scrupulously, and explaining it faithfully by divine commission and with the help of the Holy Spirit; it draws from this one deposit of faith everything which it presents for belief as divinely revealed" (DV 10).

For theologians who believe, as we do, in the infallibility of the magisterium in defining dogmas of faith, the certain identification of such a dogma calls for our act of faith in the truth that has been defined. We will share in the profession of faith that the council or pope has made in defining it. Our acceptance of the statement as a dogma of faith gives us absolute assurance *that* this truth is revealed, and hence *that* it can be found in Scripture and Tradition. However, the statement of the magisterium will rarely give a satisfactory answer to the question as to *how* it is revealed; *how* it is there in the "one deposit of faith." This is where theology enters the picture. But various answers have been given to the question as to how this particular function of theology should be understood.

I think it could be instructive if we first recall how Pope Pius XII answered this question in his 1950 encyclical *Humani generis.* There he said:

---

[8]Piet Fransen, "The Authority of Councils," in John M. Todd, ed., *Problems of Authority* (Baltimore: Helicon, 1962) 43-78.

It is likewise true that theologians must always return to the sources of divine revelation, for it is their task to show how what is taught by the living magisterium is found, whether explicitly or implicitly, in Sacred Scripture and in divine Tradition. . . . Along with these sacred fonts God has given to his church the living magisterium, for the sake of clarifying and spelling out what is contained only obscurely and implicitly in the deposit of faith . . . it is evident how wrong a method it is to explain what is clear from what is obscure; rather it is the exactly contrary procedure that all should follow. Wherefore Our Predecessor of immortal memory, Pius IX, when teaching that it is theology's most noble function to demonstrate how doctrine defined by the church is contained in the sources, not without grave reason added those words: "in the very same sense in which it has been defined." (D-S 3886).

Joseph Ratzinger expressed his dissatisfaction with this view of the role of theology in no uncertain terms, in his commentary on *Dei Verbum,* where he said;

> Thus the risk of a false orientation cannot be dismissed when *Humani generis* (which incidentally quotes Pius IX on the point) declares that it is obviously wrong to seek to clarify what is clear by the help of what is obscure—which means in the context that it is not the teaching office that can be clarified by Scripture, but only, on the contrary, Scripture by the teaching office. This is then developed to the point at which the task of theology is described as that of showing how what the teaching office has established is contained in the sources—'and that precisely in the sense in which it has been defined.' One can hardly deny that the point of view which sees only Scripture as what is unclear, but the teaching office as what is clear, is a very limited one and that to reduce the task of theology to the proof of the presence of the statements of the teaching office in the sources is to threaten the primacy of the sources which, (were one to continue logically in this direction) would ultimately destroy the serving character of the teaching office.[9]

One can hardly disagree with Ratzinger's criticism of an understanding of the role of theology that would reduce it to proving that what has been taught by the magisterium is found in the sources. Nor can it be denied that this is how Pius XII described it in this passage of *Humani generis.* However, in the interests of truth it should be noted that the earlier statement, of Pius IX, to which reference was made, was more carefully expressed. What Pius IX said was that it *pertains to* theology's most noble function to show how doctrine is contained in the sources of revelation in that very sense in which it was defined.[10] This would not so clearly *reduce* theology's role to providing such proof, as Pius XII seems to have done.

In any case, I'm sure that none of us would be satisfied with the apologetic and defensive role the two Pius's have assigned to theology here. Their statements suggest a theological method that begins with the defined dogmas, and returns to Scripture, the Fathers and early councils only in search of proof-texts that will support and defend the dogmas. In this view, the purpose of the theologian's return to the sources would be to bring the clear light of the defined dogma to illuminate the obscurities in Scripture and Tradition. What is lacking here is the

---

[9]In H. Vorgrimler, ed., *Commentary on the Documents of Vatican II,* vol. 3, (New York: Herder and Herder, 1969) 197.

[10]Pius IX, "Inter Gravissimas," Oct. 28, 1870, *Acta Pii IX* pars I, vol. 5, 260.

recognition of the primacy of the sources, and of the critical function of theology to examine the dogma itself in the light of the sources: not, to be sure, with a view to rejecting the dogma, but with a view to integrating it into the whole of revelation where alone any particular doctrine can be adequately understood.

It is the nature of a dogmatic statement to be an interpretation, in a particular context, of some particular aspect of the Word of God. In most cases the magisterium felt it was necessary to speak definitively on this particular point because it was in danger of being obscured or negated by a contemporary heresy. For this reason the dogmatic statement focused on the truth being threatened, leaving out many other related truths that did not require affirmation at the time.

However, the necessarily partial nature of any dogmatic statement can lead to one-sided and distorted interpretations, if the aspect of revealed truth which the dogma affirms is not seen against the background of the other truths with which it must be kept in proportion. Hence, one purpose of the theologian's return to the sources will be to identify the aspects of revealed truth left unspoken in the dogma, but with which the dogma has to be kept in balance, since its very truth depends on its integration into the whole of revelation. One recent example of the fruitfulness of such a return to the sources has been the reinsertion of the dogma of papal primacy into the more comprehensive doctrine of episcopal collegiality.

Another reason why the theologian's return to Scripture can shed new light on a defined dogma, and even make it obvious that we can no longer formulate the dogma in exactly the same way as it was by those who originally defined it, can be that the way the dogma was formulated reflected the way that Scripture was being interpreted at that time. For instance, there are elements in Trent's doctrine about original sin that depend on a literal interpretation of the story about Adam and Eve in Genesis. One can hardly expect the Fathers of Trent to have questioned the factual historicity of this account, including the physical descent of the whole human race from this one pair. The modern theologian then will have to examine Trent's dogmatic statements about original sin with a critical eye, in the light of the modern exegesis of Genesis, in order to discern what is permanently true in the dogma, from the elements that depend on a kind of scriptural exegesis that we can no longer practice. So the theologian returns to Scripture not just to prove that the dogma is found there, but rather, with the advantage of a better exegetical method than was available to the people who defined the dogma, to seek a better understanding of what is permanently true in the dogma itself, and to propose a more adequate way of expressing that truth.

While as men and women of faith we accept dogmatic statements with confidence in the permanent truth of their meaning, as theologians we examine the same statements critically with awareness of the historicity which they share with every human statement. Bernard Lonergan has expressed this in his typically incisive way, in the following passage from his *Method in Theology:* ''The permanence of dogmas results from the fact that they express revealed mysteries. Their historicity, on the other hand, results from the facts that (1) statements have meanings only in their contexts, and (2) contexts are ongoing and ongoing contexts are multiple. What is opposed to the historicity of the dogmas is, not their permanence, but classicist assumptions and achievements. Classicism assumed that culture was to be conceived not empirically but normatively, and it did all it could to bring about one universal, permanent culture. What ended classicist assumptions was critical history. What builds the bridges between the many expressions of the faith is a methodical theology."[11]

I think it could be instructive at this point to compare two fairly recent statements of the Roman magisterium, one of which would seem to reflect the classicist assumptions of which Lonergan speaks, while the other acknowledges the historically conditioned nature of dogmatic formulations.

The first is from Paul VI's Encyclical *Mysterium fidei* of September 3, 1965. Referring to the formulas with which the Council of Trent had expressed the dogma about the Eucharist, he declared: "By means of the formulas which the church uses in proposing dogmas of faith, concepts are expressed which are not tied to some definite human culture, to some particular level of knowledge, to one or another theological school; rather they manifest what the human mind perceives about things by universal and necessary experience, and that it expresses with appropriate and definite terms, whether derived from common or more cultivated language. For this reason, these formulas are well adapted to all men of all times and all places."[12]

Eight years after the publication of *Mysterium fidei,* and while Paul VI was still Pope, the Congregation for the Doctrine of the Faith published its Declaration entitled *Mysterium Ecclesiae,* in which, for the first time, a document of the Roman magisterium clearly recognized the historically conditioned character of dogmatic statements. The document is surely familiar to you, but it seems worthwhile to recall its key passage here, so as to bring out the newness of this approach, as compared with what we have just quoted from the papal encyclical of 1965.

Having noted that some of the difficulties which the church encounters in the transmission of divine revelation arise from the historical condition that affects the expression of revelation, the Congregation goes on to say:

> "With regard to this historical condition, it must first be observed that the meaning of the pronouncements of faith depends partly upon the expressive power of the language used at a certain point in time and in particular circumstances. Moreover, it sometimes happens that some dogmatic truth is first expressed incompletely (but not falsely), and at a later date, when considered in a broader context of faith or human knowledge, it receives a fuller and more perfect expression. . . . Finally, even though the truths which the church intends to teach through her dogmatic formulas are distinct from the changeable conceptions of a given epoch and can be expressed without them, nevertheless it can sometimes happen that these truths may be enunciated by the Sacred Magisterium in terms that bear traces of such conceptions."[13]

While the 1973 Declaration marks a welcome advance over the Encyclical of 1965, one would still share Karl Rahner's criticism of the idea that it only "sometimes happens" that the terms used in dogmatic formulas bear traces of the

---

[11]Bernard Lonergan, *Method in Theology* (New York: Herder and Herder, 1972) 326.

[12]Paul VI, "Mysterium Fidei," Sept. 3, 1965, *AAS* 57 (1965) 758.

[13]"Mysterium Ecclesiae," June 24, 1973, *AAS* 65 (1973) 402-403.

changeable concepts of a given epoch, and that they can actually be expressed without them. He remarks: "Here the authors of the document are evidently still influenced by the earlier notion of 'natural' and general human terminology, which can always and everywhere be understood without further explanation, and which is independent of the wider context of the history of thought as a whole."[14]

Obviously, much more needs to be said about the dogmatic pronouncements of the magisterium as *loci theologici,* and about theology's hermeneutical task of grasping the meaning of dogmas in their own context, and of translating that meaning into concepts and terms that are appropriate to the culture to which the theologian belongs. However, that would lead into the whole question of theological method, which is beyond the scope of this paper. So I shall move on to say something about the other kind of magisterial statements we find in Denzinger: the one described in the title as *declarationes.*

NON-DEFINITIVE TEACHING OF THE MAGISTERIUM AS A LOCUS FOR THEOLOGY

While there are other examples of this kind of teaching in Denzinger, I shall focus my remarks on papal encyclicals and doctrinal declarations of the Congregation for the Doctrine of the Faith.

In general, I believe one has to agree with Pius XII when he said in *Humani generis* that "for the most part (*plerumque*), what is proposed and insisted on in Encyclical Letters already belongs to Catholic doctrine on other grounds" (D-S 3885). A reading of the major encyclicals of the past century or so would I believe bear out the truth of this claim. This means that the formal authority of the encyclical as ordinary magisterium may be of a lesser order than the intrinsic authority of the doctrine itself, which may already be dogma of faith, whether defined solemnly or not.

The Pope's use of the word *plerumque* suggests one aspect of our role as theologians as regards papal encyclicals: to distinguish within the document between what already belongs to Catholic doctrine, possibly even to dogma, from what does not. In the light of such discernment, our response as Catholics will be appropriate to the objective weight of the doctrine itself. Our critical role as theologians will focus on the way that the papal document has conceptualized and formulated the doctrine: in other words, on the strictly theological component of this particular expression of the doctrine. It is inevitable that a certain kind of theological reflection will have gone into the way the doctrine is now being presented to the Catholic faithful. Without questioning the truth of the dogma or the well-established Catholic doctrine that is being taught, we can look critically at the theological element which, as Rahner has put it, is always part of the "amalgam" when a doctrine is conceptualized and formulated.[15] It is possible that we may find that this element reflects a theological point of view that does not take account of im-

---

[14]Karl Rahner, "Mysterium Ecclesiae," *Theological Investigations* 17 (London: Darton Longman & Todd, 1981) 149.

[15]Karl Rahner, "Magisterium and Theology," *Theological Investigations* 18 (London: Darton Longman & Todd, 1983) 54- 73.

portant developments in human knowledge. It would seem to me that in such a case, it is altogether appropriate for a Catholic theologian to express his critique of the theological component, and, as a positive contribution, to propose what he thinks would be a more satisfactory way of presenting this doctrine.

Of course it has to be kept in mind that it is no simple matter to draw the line between what in any dogma is the permanent truth which is the object of our faith, and the possibly reformable theology with which it has been conceptualized. When a theologian proposes what he has reason to believe would be a better way to understand and express a doctrine, the question may well be raised whether his new formulation does justice to the truth that is at stake. The burden of proof falls on him to show that his criticism of the official teaching only affects the theological component of the amalgam, and fully preserves the dogmatic truth involved.

Here we must point out an important difference between those statements of the magisterium which enunciate dogmatic truth, and other kinds of statements that we may find in such documents as papal encyclicals and declarations of the Congregation for the Doctrine of the Faith. When it is question of dogma, theology will enter into the statement as the form in which the dogma has been conceptualized. Any new conceptualization will intend to safeguard the permanent truth of the dogma. However, experience shows that in documents of the ordinary magisterium, statements are sometimes made where theology enters not only into the form, but into the very substance of what is being taught. In other words, a critical examination of such documents can detect the presence of what are really theological options that are being given the weight of official sanction and presented as the teaching of the magisterium.

It seems that the best one can hope for is that the theological options that are elevated to the rank of official teaching in documents of the ordinary magisterium, would reflect the best theological opinion available at the time. When this is the case, one can expect that, at the time when it is promulgated, such teaching will meet general acceptance in the theological community. Subsequently, of course, in the light of theological progress, it may become evident that a position which was adopted by the magisterium in its ordinary teaching, is no longer the best opinion available. In such a case, the ideal result would be for the magisterium to acknowledge the fact that its previous teaching was a matter of theology rather than of dogma, and to restate its doctrine in the light of the progress that has been made in the understanding of the question in the meanwhile.

However, for several reasons, there is bound to be resistance to such a revision of official teaching. First, I think it is understandably difficult for a pope to depart openly and explicitly from the teaching of his recent predecessors. A modern pope of course can easily enough acknowledge the fact that the claim of medieval popes to divinely-granted power to judge and depose temporal sovereigns was not a matter of dogma, but a theological conclusion whose minor premises are now seen to be unsound. Similarly, popes can now admit that the teaching of the Council of Florence that all pagans, Jews, heretics and schismatics would go to Hell if they did not become Catholics was based on the assumption that all such persons were guilty of the sin of infidelity, and did not necessarily follow from the dogma about the church's necessity for salvation.

However, psychologically, it seems much more difficult for a pope to correct the teaching of his recent predecessors. The natural resistance of the Roman magisterium to the correction of previous papal teaching can result in the practice of choosing consultants for future statements regarding the same issue, only from among those known to stand firm with the previous teaching. Such one- sided consultation will normally result in the reaffirmation of the previous teaching, which, because of genuine theological progress that has been made on the issue, may no longer obtain the consensus of the theological community.

I would like to suggest what I see as a concrete example of the kind of situation I am referring to here. It has to do with the kind of consultation that took place in the preparation of the *schema de Ecclesia* that was presented to the Second Vatican Council during the first period in 1962. As is well known, the Preparatory Theological Commission that was responsible for this *schema* was dominated by the then Holy Office, with its Prefect, Cardinal Ottaviani, as its head, and Fr. Sebastian Tromp, a leading consultor to the Holy Office, as its secretary. The selection of theologians to be named to this Commission, and the extent to which some who were named were actually listened to, reflected the kind of theology that characterized the Holy Office during the 1950's.

One of the basic assumptions of this theology, as one can see from the references given in the notes to the *schema*,[16] was that the council would in no respect depart from the official positions already taken by the popes in their encyclicals.[17] Theologians who had expressed criticism of any such papal teaching had no significant role in the preparation of this *schema*.

We know what happened when the bishops came to Rome for the council, with theologians of their own choosing, and went to work on that preparatory *schema*. It met with such a negative reception that it was withdrawn without even being put to a vote. In the course of the next two years, the council hammered out a dogmatic constitution on the church that, while not perfect, and surely not the last word, has deservedly been well received by the theological community. On a number of significant issues, it does depart from what had been previous papal teaching: departures that were accepted and confirmed by the papal magisterium in the person of Pope Paul VI.

In his book, *The Papacy and the Church*,[18] J. Robert Dionne has examined in painstaking detail the process that led up to the acceptance by Paul VI of the reversal of previous papal teaching on such issues as the Catholic attitude to non-Christian religions, church-state relations, and religious liberty, as well as the ecclesiological issues of church identity and church membership. After demonstrating the sometimes neglected fact that the reception of papal teaching in the Catholic Church, from the time of Pius IX to the end of the Second Vatican Council, was

---

[16]*Acta Synodalia Concilii Vaticani Secundi* I/4 (Vatican City: Typis Polyglottis Vaticanis, 1971) 16-91.

[17]Umberto Betti, "Chiesa di Cristo e Chiesa Cattolica," *Antonianum* 61 (1986) 726-45.

[18]J. Robert Dionne, *The Papacy and the Church. A Study of Praxis and Reception in Ecumenical Perspective* (New York: Philosophical Library, 1987).

predominantly positive, he goes on to show that on those five issues, it was the critical reception by some Catholic theologians that had brought to light the fact that a position at variance with the official teaching was more solidly embedded in Catholic tradition than the official position was. It was the recognition of this fact that eventually brought about the consensus at Vatican II in favor of the change.

Dionne's thesis, then, is that recent history proves that the development of doctrine in the Catholic Church is not a one-directional affair, of authentic teaching by the magisterium and unquestioning assent by the rest of the church. Rather, it involves the interplay of authoritative teaching, and the reception of this teaching by the church. While this reception will normally be positive, it sometimes includes "respectful and responsible 'talking back' " on the part of Catholic theologians,[19] which can lead to the acceptance of a change of position on the part of the papal magisterium itself.

I believe that Dionne's thesis is correct. The question I would raise, however, is whether he has given sufficient consideration to the fact that it required the extraordinary event of an ecumenical council to make possible the broad consultation of the whole church that resulted in the differences between the teaching of Vatican II and that of previous papal encyclicals. Reflecting on the kind of doctrine we find in the *schemata* prepared by the Preparatory Theological Commission, I feel justified in doubting whether the ordinary magisterium of the Holy See would have been likely to undertake any such revision of papal teaching if it had not been exposed to the fresh ideas brought to Rome by the bishops and their theologians. One can only hope that in the preparation of important doctrinal statements, the Holy See would not repeat the mistake made by the preparatory commission, but rather follow the example of the council, where the bishops listened to all shades of Catholic theological opinion before coming to their judgment. What the council has demonstrated is that even theological opinion that is critical of papal teaching deserves a fair hearing, and can lead the church to a better grasp of its own tradition. I suggest that this is what the bishops had in mind when they declared that "all the faithful, clerical and lay, possess a lawful freedom of inquiry and of thought, and the freedom to express their minds humbly and courageously about those matters in which they enjoy competence" (GS 62).

FRANCIS A. SULLIVAN, SJ
Gregorian University

---

[19]Dionne, *Papacy and Church,* 292.

A RESPONSE TO FRANCIS SULLIVAN

It is difficult to formulate a critical response to Francis Sullivan's paper. To be sure, I owe him the respect of a former student at the Pontifical Gregorian University at the time of the Second Vatican Council. And that respect I freely and gladly offer him. But the deeper root of the difficulty is that I can find little of substance in his paper with which to take issue. On the contrary, it is at once clear, coherent, balanced, and generally forthright—by which I mean that it makes some effort to apply principles to practice, with examples.

Of course, I could share with you an outline of the paper *I* might have delivered here today, but that would be yielding to the perennial temptation of respondents and reviewers; namely, to transform one's role from interpreter to competitor. I shall not do that.

What I shall do instead is simply italicize points and arguments that I find particularly pertinent to, and illuminating of, the ongoing discussion concerning the relationship between the hierarchical magisterium and theology. (I use the adjective "hierarchical" deliberately here, because it is clear that Father Sullivan's paper intends to restrict the discussion to that level and form of magisterium). Before doing so, however, I should mention just three items that the paper might also have addressed explicitly; namely, the meaning and import of ordinary universal magisterium (how it is determined and how the authority of its formulations differs from that of definitive, or dogmatic, pronouncements); secondly, some indication of the pertinence of the current debate over national episcopal conferences and *their* teaching authority, or *mandatum docendi;* and, thirdly, the role of reception in the magisterial process. Sullivan does make some mention of reception in his brief discussion of J. Robert Dionne's *The Papacy and the Church.* Moreover, he treats universal ordinary magisterium and reception in his *Magisterium: Teaching Authority in the Catholic Church* (New York: Paulist Press, 1983).

The threefold division of authoritative documents in Denzinger's *Enchiridion Symbolorum, Definitionum Declarationum* provides the structure for this paper: first, baptismal creeds; secondly, solemn definitions; and, thirdly, a variety of nondefinitive statements, or declarations, of the hierarchical magisterium.

Sullivan insists that the baptismal creeds "constitute a primary *locus* for theology" because they "witness to the way the apostolic faith was handed on from generation to generation in the churches." In a sense, he suggests, "the major purpose of all subsequent interventions of the magisterium has been to explicitate, clarify and defend the true sense in which various articles of the baptismal creed are to be understood."

Indeed, the hierarchical magisterium first got involved in the business of formulating doctrines, not for reasons of control but for reasons of sacramental initiation and of worship. The earliest professions of faith were used in the baptismal and then the eucharistic liturgies, not in loyalty oaths and heresy trials. Had the hierarchical magisterium remained faithful to its original liturgical partner and not set it aside for a new canonical partner, the history of the relationship between the hierarchical magisterium and theology might have been different.

Sullivan reminds us that there was no single creed agreed upon by all and employed by all. Put a late 20th-century traditional Catholic in a time machine and send her or him back into the second or third centuries with the assignment of retrieving a copy of "the Creed," and such a Catholic would return perplexed and empty-handed. Important, if not novel, points.

I do raise one parenthetical question here about Father Sullivan's apparent interpretation of the *credo ecclesiam* of the baptismal profession. He seems to place on equal footing, as the object of Christian faith, the *ecclesiam* which is "the fruit of Christ's definitive victory over the powers of evil . . . [with] the abiding presence of the Holy Spirit" and, on the other hand, "the episcopal and papal structure of the Catholic Church [corresponding] to God's design for his church." The latter may be *implied* in the former, but there is no ecclesiological parity between the two, as the text of the paper might otherwise suggest. The papal-episcopal structure of the church is, at most, an inference of faith, not its object.

One begins to feel the real force of Sullivan's paper as the presentation moves from baptismal creeds to definitions and declarations. How does one distinguish between the two? What is the difference between definitive, or infallible, teachings, and non-definitive, or non-infallible, teachings? To pose the question is already to concede the distinction. Francis Sullivan accepts the distinction as a matter of course, in concert with most other Catholic theologians. The challenge is to discern the line that separates definitions from declarations. Indeed, Sullivan argues that this challenge is a "primary task of theology;" namely, "to establish the criteria by which defined dogmas can be distinguished from all other statements of doctrine." Although Sullivan does not say it, that is precisely the point at issue in Charles Curran's recent disagreement with Cardinal Ratzinger and other ecclesiastical officials. Curran, like Sullivan, insists on the distinction. The latter tend to collapse it, or to expand the territory occupied by definitive statements through a liberal appeal to ordinary universal magisterium, thereby creating a 1980's version of "creeping infallibilism." (Indeed, it is at this point in the paper that the neglect of the question of ordinary universal magisterium is most keenly felt.)

With a supporting citation from the same Joseph Ratzinger, Father Sullivan identifies the central flaw in the papal-curial understanding of theology during the pre-Vatican II period, and particularly during the pontificate of Pius XII; namely, its assumption that theology exists to clarify what is in the sources of revelation by flooding them with the light of dogma. In other words, the task of theology is reduced to "proving that what has been taught by the magisterium is found in the sources." Sullivan does not say so, but this view of theology perdures not only at the hierarchical level, but also among many whose theological credentials are either self-conferred or bestowed by the media. Many of these theologians without portfolio populate departments of philosophy in various Catholic colleges and universities.

On the contrary, Sullivan argues, the theologian's task is to examine dogmas in the light of the sources, not the sources in the light of dogmas. One reason among several why the theologian returns to the sources is to "identify the aspects of revealed truth left unspoken in the dogma" and then to integrate those aspects into the whole of revelation.

Following not only Karl Rahner and Bernard Lonergan but also the Vatican declaration *Mysterium Ecclesiae,* Sullivan insists on the historically conditioned character of all dogmatic formulations, citing unfortunate instances of non-historical, classicist thinking in recent magisterial pronouncements, including Pope Paul VI's encyclical on the Eucharist, *Mysterium fidei.*

Francis Sullivan's paper moves, in a third and final section, to a discussion of non-definitive declarations of the hierarchical magisterium, particularly those contained in papal encyclicals and the pronouncements of the Congregation for the Doctrine of the Faith.

Within such documents, he insists, the theologian must distinguish "between what already belongs to Catholic doctrine, possibly even to dogma, from what does not." For Sullivan, it is "altogether appropriate for a Catholic theologian to express his critique of the theological component" of a non-definitive teaching, and "to propose what he thinks would be a more satisfactory way of presenting this doctrine."

It is almost inevitable, he implies, that such documents will have a theological component because of the role that theologians normally play as consultants in the production of these documents.

"The natural resistance of the Roman magisterium to the correction of theological options taken in previous papal teaching," he writes, "can result in the practice of choosing consultants for future statements . . . only from those who are known to stand firm with the previous teaching." He cites the preparation of the Vatican II schema on the church by way of example. When the rest of the bishops and *their* theological advisers arrived for the council, however, the schema was rejected and a new one was hammered out over the next two years.

Francis Sullivan concludes with the hope that "in the preparation of important doctrinal statements, the Holy See would not repeat the mistake made by the preparatory commission, but rather follow the example of the council, where all the bishops listened to all shades of theological opinion before coming to their judgment." Given the consistent practice of the present papal administration, however, he probably hopes in vain. One can cite the total exclusion of such theologians as Richard McCormick from the process of drafting the recent Vatican statement on reproductive technology as only the most recent case in point.

As long as this situation perdures, theologians must continue to fulfill their proper critical function by pointing out what they see as the limitations and even errors of the theology that underlies some of the positions taken by the hierarchical magisterium.

Sullivan cites article 62 of *Gaudium et spes* in support of his modest hope; namely, that "all the faithful, clerical and lay, possess a lawful freedom of inquiry and of thought, and the freedom to express their minds humbly and courageously about those matters in which they enjoy competence.''

But *Gaudium et spes* is out of favor these days with many who have responsibility for shaping the very policy Sullivan implicitly criticizes. Therefore, Father Sullivan might have been better advised to appeal to what some would regard as a ''higher'' authority than the council; namely, canons 212 and 218 of the new Code of Canon Law.

RICHARD P. MCBRIEN
University of Notre Dame

Presidential Address

LANGUAGE AND PRAXIS:
RECENT THEOLOGICAL TRENDS

By definition as a presidential address is a "period piece." In 1953 the Board
of Directors of the Society determined that the presidential address should be "a
summary of the theological progress of the year, or a period of time, or recent
theological developments and trends, a kind of general conspectus of the field."[1]
This address will attempt to focus recent theological developments and trends which
might provide a kind of general conspectus of the field.

The phrase, "recent theological trends," is evocative. Is there something going
forward in present theology that might be named without "nailing it down?" Is
there something happening *a tergo* in contemporary theology, something behind
all the recent "turns," those horizon shifts initially so enthusiastically embraced
but whose regulative authority waned so swiftly as theologians discovered the
limitations of their paradigmatic sweep? The "turn to the subject" was exhila-
rating. It retrieved the ideal language of the person, history as human time, consciousness and freedom in celebration of the "infinite outreach" of the human
spirit. With the first phase of the modern Enlightenment this turn was optimistic,
and the Vatican II spirit of *Gaudium et spes* caught the contagion of its enthusi-
asm. But how soon it ended! People took a second look at its assertions and realized that they were formulated in an "optative mood." Let us take just one
example—the Rahnerian interpretation of history as the field of freedom, the self-
enactment of the human person, with eternity as its future fruit. This notion of
history cannot be dismissed as an illustration of Rahnerian "optimism." It is but
the theological interpretation of history which flows from an historically con-
scious retrieval of the reality of grace in accord with the Catholic tradition. When
one moves from this vision of divine grace as efficacious in human history to the
concrete realities of current history, however, one finds the latter in obvious conflict with the former vision of how things should be. A complementary development is necessary whereby this theological interpretation of history must be made
real in the actual reality of history.

In response to this recognition that "things are not the way they should be,"
there emerged the "socio-political turn" to the primacy of *praxis* over theory with
a new sense of urgency that theology must now be "realized." With the spread
of this sense of urgency there developed in rapid succession Continental political
theology, Latin American liberation theology, and North American liberation theologies. In general, this new political theology defined itself as complementary

[1]*CTSA Proceedings* 8 (1953) 174.

to, as a necessary corrective of, former personalist and existential theologies. The forces inimical to authentic history, religious privatism, massive poverty, sexism, racism, etc. were named, and the *praxis* of emancipation was enjoined on all Christians in the name of the liberating God of the Exodus and Jesus.

In this turn from the personal subject to the political situation theology retained its general "method of correlation," but the range of its employment was expanded from the focus of the cognitive or conative subject in quest of authenticity to the structures of the social world of the late twentieth century as overpowering obstacles to authentic human existence for the majority of the human race. Toward overcoming the global forces of alienation the meaning and truth of the gospel had to be correlated with the praxiological necessity of "changing the world." While existential or transcendential theology placed the emphasis on personal faith, the *fides qua creditur,* as explicit or implicit, political and liberation theologies have reclaimed the traditional primacy of doctrinal faith, the *fides quae creditur,* as the source of the Christian vision of emancipation. Thus, the Exodus portrayal of the liberating God and the memory of Jesus, the Liberator, become the energizing biblical symbols for Christian *praxis* in and for the world. If the former theology sought to interpret the person in light of the gospel, the new theology would serve the practical transformation of human society. In its exuberance this new political theology seemed to forget the human subject in its attempt to overcome privatism and individualism, but it did bring a pervasive awareness that *praxis* sublates theory, while theory arises from and seeks to serve *praxis.*

It is interesting to note how theologians have refused to translate the Greek word, *praxis,* into English. The problem here is the current ambiguity of the word, practice. It could mean something like "applied theory," or it could be understood in our technological age as a synonym for production. To retrieve its authentic meaning philosophers and theologians leave the word untranslated. To clarify its meaning the philosophers and theologians have to return to Aristotle's clarification of the three realms of human being in the world; 1) the realm of *theoria* in search of *epistēmē;* 2) the realm of *praxis* in quest of *phronēsis;* and 3) the realm of *poiesis* in need of *technē.*

For a time the new insistence on the primacy of *praxis* took the form of programmatic essays, strongly exhortative in style but rather vague as to details. Both the Aristotelian and the Hegelian-Marxist traditions on *praxis* were retrieved to formulate what is distinctive about human ethical and political action. Eventually the question of what constituted specifically Christian *praxis* had to be faced. Thus did the rediscovery of the primacy of *praxis* in political theology lead to a new "turn" in contemporary theology—the "linguistic turn." For the answer to the question of what Christian faith brings to emancipatory *praxis* demanded a new look at the Christian tradition, a tradition (like all human traditions) which is linguistically constituted.

At this point some theologians were brought to a new awareness of what their traditional dialogue partners, the philosophers, were doing. These theologians discovered that "language has emerged as a prominent, perhaps the predominant, philosophical and intellectual concern in our century."[2] This philosophy of lan-

---

[2]Fred R. Dallmayr, *Polis and Praxis* (Cambridge, MA: The MIT Press, 1984) 192.

guage has developed in two distinct forms, the Anglo- American linguistic analysis and the Continental hermeneutical phenomenology. Linguistic analysis was for a time a form of positivism, and there was little contact between this approach to language and that of the European hermeneutical tradition. This situation has begun to change, and significant communication between the two ''schools'' is in motion. In the meantime, contemporary theology has been deeply affected by the hermeneutical tradition.

There is no need for us to rehearse again the modern history of hermeneutics from Schleiermacher to Dilthey to Heidegger to Gadamer.[3] In terms of the new ''practical interests'' of theologians the thought of Gadamer is of considerable import. For Gadamer's central concern is the retrieval of tradition as the historical mediation of meaning and value for the *praxis* of human life. Under the influence of Gadamer theology becomes the hermeneutics of the Christian tradition. Critiqued by the Enlightenment as the carrier of heteronomous constriant, tradition has been ''vindicated'' in our day by the work of Gadamer, Ricoeur, *et al*.[4] Instructed by Heidegger's notion of the initial importance of our ''pre- understanding.'' Gadamer has rehabilitated the word, ''prejudice.'' Against the Enlightenment's ''prejudice against prejudices'' Gadamer shows that we are constituted as historical beings far more by our ''prejudices'' (pre-judgments appropriated spontaneously from our living traditions) than by our judgments.[5] Tradition has an ''effective history'' as it continues to constitute human consciousness, and this power of tradition testifies to the power of language since tradition is itself primarily linguistic.

In his concern to understand understanding Gadamer distinguishes three ''moments'' in the process: 1) the enabling elements in our prejudices; 2) interpretation as a ''fusion of horizons;'' and 3) ''application.'' Of the three the last is the most important for the practical interest of hermeneutical phenomenology, for it is the ''moment'' of application that brings Gadamer into conversation with the practical philosophy of Aristotle. While Aristotelian metaphysics as the clearest illustration of Greek cosmocentrism had long ago given way to the modern philosophies of the subject, the practical legacy of the Philosopher now instructs those who would overcome modern ''subjectivism'' through the investigation of the most ''intersubjective'' phenomenon of all, language.

The Latin translation of Aristotle's anthropology, the *animal rationale*, clearly illustrates the traditional Western emphasis on the cognitive capacity as the characteristically human trait. The famous *cogito* of Descartes is a perfect symbol of the Western perception of the human being as defined by the power of reason, thought, knowledge. As this Western ideal of the solitary thinker who uses language to share with others the fruits of private thought begins to wane in our day, it is refreshing to take a new look at Aristotle's famous definition of the human

[3]See Richard E. Palmer, *Hermeneutics: Interpretation Theory in Schleiermacher, Dilthey, Heidegger, and Gadamer* (Evanston: Northwestern University Press, 1969).

[4]On this retrieval of tradition see Jaroslav Pelikan, *The Vindication of Tradition* (New Haven: Yale University Press, 1984).

[5]Hans-Georg Gadamer, *Truth and Method* (New York: Crossroad, 1982) 239-40.

being in the original Greek, *to zoon ton logon echōn,* "the speaking animal."[6] Perhaps, then, Aristotle cannot be blamed for the tradition (mis)understanding of language in the West as "instrumental" or "expressive" of pre-linguistic thoughts. Thinking follows language. Language enables thinking. One may speak of "pre-conceptual" experience, as long as "pre-conceptual" does not mean "pre- linguistic." Human experience is always already "interpreted" experience, and the interpretation witnesses to the linguistic potential of the tradition that has always already formed a human consciousness. Pre-linguistic experience is pre-human experience. The spontaneously engendered symbolic structuring of consciousness describes every human being as a finite, historical, and social reality. For anyone linguistic competence is primarily a practical competence enabling participation in the various "forms of life" which describe an historical people. Theologians today seem to concur in asserting the primacy of *praxis* over theory, but this recognition requires further elaboration in terms of elucidating just what constitutes *praxis* as human action, ethical or political. The reflective turn from the "theorizing subject" to the praxiologically engaged community of subjects is incomplete without the "linguistic turn" which discovers that what renders *praxis praxis* (human) is that intersubjective web which binds a people together in an ongoing "conversation." In replacing the category, substance, with the Subject Hegel discerned "the cunning of Reason" active "behind our backs" in the drama of history. Today we might replace this "cunning of Reason" with "the cunning of the Word," for "in the beginning was the Word."

Reflection on language is reflection on reality as rendered perceptible, intelligible, and "unfinished." Language liberates us from the limitations of an environment for that intersubjective reality was call "the world." The world is effected by the word as human beings reveal their humanity in naming things. This naming is the primordial human *praxis* of "the image and likeness" of God who created the world through the divine Word. Just as God's eternal expressibility is the origin of everything that exists, so human expressibility is the origin of history. We are like God because we can speak. Indeed, we are so like God that when God spoke God to us "speaking animals," our humanity supplied the grammar for the divine self-utterance.[7]

LEXIS AND PRAXIS

Language as the symbolic structuring of the imagination produces the human being as a thinking and acting being in the world. Just as language "gives rise to thought," so also language empowers *praxis*. This empowerment cannot be reduced to the simplistic imperative, "think and act." The knowing that guides *praxis* is a special kind of knowing commonly referred to as *phronēsis*. *Phronēsis* is the spontaneously employed but habitually present practical "know how" of the morally responsible person. The recent retrieval of the Aristotelian virtue of *phro-*

---

[6]See Hans-Georg Gadamer, "Man and Language" in *Philosophical Hermeneutics* (Berkeley: University of California Press) 59.

[7]See Karl Rahner, "On the Theology of the Incarnation," *Theological Investigations* 4 (Baltimore: Helicon Press, 1966) 105-20.

nēsis signals a salutary departure from a notion of reason which stresses its "theoretical" or "abstract" nature whereby it is literally "drawn away from" the concrete circumstances of life. The object of *phronēsis* is always concrete. It cannot be anticipated in abstraction from the concrete circumstances of its enactment.[8] This "cardinal virtue" on which hinges the entire reality of *praxis* is the fruit of sustained self-determination through critically reflective appropriation of values mediated by the living tradition of one's community. Tradition is linguistically effective in the formation of the imagination of people within its pale, and this formation nourishes the development of *phronēsis*—to the extent that the tradition itself is a carrier of authentic values.

One of the clearest illustrations of the linguistic formation of the virtue of *phronēsis* is the practical role of narrative in human societies. The intrinsically temporal character of human existence finds its most appropriate symbolization in the mimetic character of narrative. Indeed, as Paul Ricoeur insists, "time becomes human to the extent that it is articulated through a narrative mode, and narrative attains its full meaning when it becomes a condition of temporal existence."[9] The classic narratives of a people give them their identity and specify their tasks by telling stories of persons and events that reveal the meaning and value of human life. Through hearing these narratives people are gradually brought to active participation in their communities by a kind of "osmosis." The linguistic tradition of the community works ideally to the extent that it continues to effect the virtue of *phronēsis*.

But tradition, like everything human, is ambiguous. The heteronomous power of tradition was uncovered by the Enlightenment's call to autonomy by way of courageous rejection of the trammels of the past. Tradition was identified with bondage. Today, however, as was said above, we witness a certain "vindication" of tradition, a renewal of a guarded trust in its power to mediate authentic values. While the thought of Gadamer testifies to the positive value of tradition, Ricoeur has shown that any retrieval of the authentic human possibilities mediated by tradition must be forged by way of a detour through a "hermeneutics of suspicion." Accordingly, any renewal of the virtue of *phronēsis* demands a critical attitude toward the tradition which transmits the shared values of the community wherein alone is *phronēsis* a real possibility. This crisis of tradition affects all traditions as formative of all communities, and thus the Christian tradition as formative of the Christian community.

The Christian community has its own understanding of *phronēsis*. Paul exhorted the community at Phillipi with the words, *"Touto phroneite. . . .* Have this (Christ's) attitude in you" (Phil 2:5).[10] The community must appropriate the *phronēsis* of Christ. Now this Christian *phronēsis* is identical with discipleship,

---

[8]See Paul Giurlanda, *Faith and Knowledge: A Critical Inquiry* (Lanham, MD: University Press of America, 1987) 76-97.

[9]Paul Ricoeur, *Time and Narrative,* 3 vols. (Chicago: The University of Chicago Press, 1984) 1:52.

[10]This Epistle employs the verb, *phronein,* and its derivitives ten times; see *Noveau Testament, Traduction Oecuménique de la Bible* (Paris: Les Editions du Cerf, 1975) 588, fn. k.

literally learning one's "know how" from personal apprenticeship to Jesus in that "school of apprentices" formed by its memory of Jesus, the community called church. For Paul *phronēsis* is the practical wisdom that flows from *charis,* the grace of Christ which is the presence of the Spirit in the church (Eph 1:8). This practical wisdom is learned by living in the symbolically structured (predominantly narrative symbols!) society wherein Jesus, God's Speech, is heard in the power of the Spirit. As a religious tradition, faithfully transmitted from generation to generation over almost two millennia, the Christian tradition is identical with the lived sense of faith of the People of God. With focus on the *praxis* of discipleship this lived sense of faith is identical with the virtue of *phronēsis,* translated by St. Thomas as *prudentia,* the *recta ratio agibilium,* but untranslated by us (for reasons similar to our refusal to translated *praxis*)—the English word, prudence, is often reduced to something like "cautious calculation."

Perhaps the most prominent illustration of the "linguistic turn" in contemporary theology is narrative theology. Here we will reflect on narrative theologies as "exercises in understanding, assessing, and proclaiming a religious tradition which take stories as conceptually prior to doctrinal formulations of theological systematization, for these could not make sense without a narrative context."[11] In a recent article on the *status quo* of narrative theology Gary Comstock distinguishes between two kinds of contemporary narrative theologians, the "purists" and the "impurists."[12] For the "purists" the entire theological task is covered by the employment of the literary form of narrative theology as over against any use of the conceptual abstractions traditionally characteristic of systematic theology. Pure narrative theology, as such, without any "ancillary discipline," can accomplish the three specific theological tasks Comstock specifies: description, explanation, and justification. Narrative offers the best description; good narrative provides the only appropriate explanations; and justification is identical with the authentic *praxis* of faith formed by narrative. The "impurists," on the other hand show their "impurity" by insisting that the power of the Biblical narratives is complemented by the procedures of foundational theology which seeks a more general ground for describing the Christian faith. Again, in explaining Christianity the "impurists" do not hesitate to use the abstract language of metaphysics (for most of them today, a "metaphysics of the subject") despite the "reductionistic" tendencies of all attempts to cast the particular within a universal framework. Finally, for the "impurists" the rational justification of Christian claims demands a theoretical attempt to check the correspondence between these claims and "common human experience." Comstock's evaluation of this serious disharmony among narrative theologians is interesting: the "purists" are right about description; explanation is a "toss up;" and the "impurists" are right about justification.[13] Comstock's report on the present state of narrative theology is clear and helpful. But perhaps another report from a different perspective might further

---

[11]T. W. Tilley, "Narrative Theology" in J. Komonchak, M. Collins, and D. Lane, eds., *The New Dictionary of Theology* (Wilmington: Michael Glazier, Inc., 1987) 702.

[12]Gary Comstock, "Two Types of Narrative Theology," *Journal of the American Academy of Religion* LV (1987) 687-717.

[13]Ibid., 698, 703, 710.

clarify the actualities and the possibilities of contemporary, linguistically self-aware theology.

THE NEW JESUS LANGUAGE.

An obvious characteristic of our present theological situation is the recent focus on Jesus as "the human face of God."[14] A new "theocentric Christology" is emerging in which the long tutelage of Athens over Jerusalem is yielding to a vision of God as disclosed in Jesus. A "Jesus-shaped" God is currently reshaping everything in the church, and this new theocentrism is central to all contemporary projects of liberation and emancipation.[15]

The new forms of narrative theology have themselves been deeply affected by the Gospel accounts of the words, deeds, and destiny of Jesus. Current sensitivity to the *kind of language* found in the Gospels is transforming theological language. Very common in contemporary theological publications is the distinction between the originary or primary religious language (the language of worship and proclamation, cognate to the language of the Gospels) and the second-level language of theological discourse. At times this distinction takes the form of the contrast between the primary language *of* faith as over against the secondary language *about* faith.[16] This contrast is initially helpful, but it needs significant nuancing. Theological language must never forget that it takes its *exitus* from the primary religious language only to make its *reditus* to that language after it has performed its ancillary service of critical clarification. Theology must never model itself on Hegel's "owl of Minerva" who flies at dusk into the stratosphere of abstract universals. Theological discourse must always purchase a "return ticket" so that it never wanders too far away from the concrete particularities of the language *of* faith. In his therapy for thinking Ludwig Wittgenstein averred that "the source of philosophical problems is the betwitchment of our minds by language."[17] In constructing their "systems" theologians have at times suffered a similar bewitchment. If, as Ricoeur tells us, "the symbol gives rise to thought," that thought should as far as possible resemble its origin—if it wants to avoid gnostic pretensions.

Jean Ladrière, our keynote speaker at last year's convention, offers a further suggestion on the close relationship between religious language and theological discourse. Ladrière holds that both forms of language, the symbolic and the conceptual, share the same "semantic aim."[18] Because these different languages share the same aim, "there is an original contribution of theological reflection which

---

[14]See J. A. T. Robinson, *The Human Face of God* (London: SCM Press, 1973).

[15]See Paul Lakeland, *Freedom in Christ* (New York: Fordham University Press, 1986) 8.

[16]For an illustration of this distinction see Clodovis Boff, *Theology and Praxis* (Maryknoll: Orbis Books, 1987) 109-31.

[17]John K. Downey, *Beginning at the Beginning: Wittgenstein and Theological Conversation* (Lanham, MD: University Press of America, 1986) 87.

[18]Jean Ladrière, "Le discours théologique et le symbol," *Revue des sciences réligieuses* 49 (19) 1-2: 116-41.

adds a particular dimension to the religious language as such and thus in a certain sense makes this very language more revealing for the human mind.''[19] Thus does Ladrière help us address a common and quite serious critique of theological discourse, i.e., that it is always reductionistic. When theologians give in to that craving for generality that produces metaphysics, they cannot help but reduce the concrete particularities of the Christian story to illustrations of some universal essence. Some critics, not necessarily opposed to the second level language of theology, feel that ''reduction'' may not be all that bad, ''because 'reduction' is precisely what explanations are supposed to do.''[20] It is at this point that Ladrière's approach is most significant. To the extent that theology, the hermeneutics of the primary symbols of the faith, is able to secure its identity as serving the same semantic aim as those symbols, it will not succumb to the temptation to reduce the religious symbol system to a grand speculative scheme. Such schemes are ''bewitching'' in their effect and seductive in their siren call.

In 1926 Alfred North Whitehead claimed that ''Christianity . . . has always been a religion seeking a metaphysic. . . . ''[21] Some theologians today are happy to hear of ''the end of metaphysics'' or ''the end of ontotheology.'' They insist that, given the enormous influence of the metaphysical tradition on Christian theology, we must now await ''a new language of faith.''[22] Narrative theology is a good illustration of the emergence of this new language. Recalling the traits of expressive language elaborated by Philip Wheelwright, one might suggest that theological language, faithful to its source in Biblical symbolism, should seek relative adequacy by undergoing a transformation, a detachment from the traditional horizon of the primacy of theory through a ''reinscription'' in the horizon of the religious experience it seeks to understand—thereby contributing to the semantic aim of the primary language of faith fully aware of its own secondary but quite significant role.[23] Whitehead in the same paragraph cited above lamented that ''Christianity has, in its historical development, struggled with another difficulty, namely, the fact that it has no clear-cut separation from the crude fancies of the older tribal religions.''[24] We may wish this ''difficulty'' long life!

For the justification of the truth claims of Christianity Comstock gave the prize to the ''impurists.''[25] But even in so doing he observed that the impurist's critical correlations between religion and culture will be slight. ''Logical argumentation rarely serves the church as well as self-sacrificial service of others.''[26] The real

[19]Ladrière, ''Meaning and Truth in Theology,'' *CTSA Proceedings* 42 (1987) 12.

[20]Comstock, ''Two Types of Narrative Theology,'' 710.

[21]Alfred North Whitehead, *Religion in the Making* (Cleveland: The World Publishing Company, 1960) 50.

[22]Joseph S. O'Leary, *Questioning Back: The Overcoming of Metaphysics in Christian Tradition* (Minneapolis: Winston Press, 1985) 27.

[23]See Jean Ladrière, ''Meaning and Truth in Theology,'' 14; for ''the traits of expressive language'' see P. Wheelwright, *The Burning Fountain* (Bloomington: Indiana University Press, 1968) 73-101.

[24]Whitehead, *Religion in the Making,* 50.

[25]Comstock, ''Two Types of Narrative Theology,'' 710.

[26]Ibid., 710.

mediation or correlation occurs in *praxis*. That gift of grace which is Christian *phronēsis*, so essential for discipleship, becomes effective primarily through the linguistic power of the tradition actualized in worship. But this efficacy is also promoted in a secondary but significant way by that understanding of faith which only good theology can provide.

THE CUNNING OF LOGOS

It seems that what was happening behind our backs more or less throughout this century is that we have become more and more aware of the mystery of language as the manifestation of our common humanity. The "turn to the cognitive/conative subject" and the "political turn" have been sublated by the "linguistic turn" which has mediated our practical intersubjectivity as finite, historical beings responsible for our common world. The positive moments in these two sublations can be described as a contemporary "return to the subject" in grateful appreciation of the work of Karl Rahner: 1) the turn to the subject is taken up into the "communal subject" or "the community of *phronēsis*" of the socio-political turn; and 2) similarly, the linguistic turn empowers the socio- political turn by providing access to the *fides quae* ("orthodoxy") and accentuating communal *phronēsis* as the *fides qua* ("orthopraxy").[27]

We have come to see the interconnection of hermeneutics, *phronēsis,* and *praxis* in a community shaped by a tradition. In our contemporary Catholic community we have become critical of the presence of ideological elements which continue to legitimate the illegitimate embodiments of the memory of Christ. This critical recognition has issued in conflict within our community, and a community while in conflict over the interpretation of its tradition cannot easily promote Christian *phronēsis*. Perhaps what we need at this moment can be called a kind of *meta-phronēsis* to create the kind of environment wherein our conversation can continue.[28] The sign of this *meta-phronēsis* is civility or that respect which "stands as the cardinal virtue in both the political and the moral domains."[29]

Lest these final observations be interpreted as merely exhortations I am happy to report to the members of this Society that we are considered a model of civility and mutual respect by our Belgian keynoter of the 1987 convention. He told me how impressed he was by the congenial atmosphere of our convention sessions, an atmosphere that enhanced the rigor of our theological discussions. And from others I have learned that Professor Ladrière is spreading this good word abroad. Perhaps the right path from deconstruction to reconstruction, from the hermeneutics of suspicion to the hermeneutics of retrieval goes by way of what a recent book describes as a "hermeneutics of empathy."[30] As we continue to converse with

---

[27]For a current "retrieval of subjectivity" see Gregory Baum, *Theology and Society* (New York: Paulist Press, 1987) 261- 84.

[28]See John Caputo, *Radical Hermeneutics* (Bloomington: Indiana University Press, 1987) 262.

[29]Bernard P. Dauenhauer, *The Politics of Hope* (New York: Routledge & Kegan Paul, 1986) 95.

[30]Karl F. Morrison, *"I Am You": The Hermeneutics of Empathy in Western Literature, Theology, and Art* (Princeton: Princeton University Press, 1988).

one another empathetically, we may trust in the "cunning of the Word," that Speech which enfolds us and has much to unfold to us as we "exchange eyes for ears" in attentive listening.[31]

MICHAEL J. SCANLON, O.S.A.
Washington Theological Union

---

[31]The phrase, "to exchange eyes for ears," is an inversion of Blumenberg's thesis that exchanging ears for eyes describes Hellenization as "the transposition of biblical expressions involving hearing into ones involving sight." See Hans Blumenberg, *The Legitimacy of the Modern Age* (Cambridge: MIT Press, 1983) 286.